THE GREAT PHYSICIAN'S

R^x *for*

HIGH BLOOD PRESSURE

JORDAN RUBIN

with Joseph Brasco, M.D.

THOMAS NELSON
Since 1798

NASHVILLE   DALLAS   MEXICO CITY   RIO DE JANEIRO   BEIJING

Every effort has been made to make this book as accurate as possible. The purpose of this book is to educate. It is a review of scientific evidence that is presented for information purposes. No individual should use the information in this book for self-diagnosis, treatment, or justification in accepting or declining any medical therapy for any health problems or diseases. No individual is discouraged from seeking professional medical advice and treatment, and this book is not supplying medical advice.

Any application of the information herein is at the reader's own discretion and risk. Therefore, any individual with a specific health problem or who is taking medications must first seek advice from his personal physician or health-care provider before starting a health and wellness program. The author and Thomas Nelson Publishers, Inc., shall have neither liability nor responsibility to any person or entity with respect to loss, damage, or injury caused or alleged to be caused directly or indirectly by the information contained in this book. We assume no responsibility for errors, inaccuracies, omissions, or any inconsistency herein.

In view of the complex, individual nature of health problems, this book and the ideas, programs, procedures, and suggestions herein are not intended to replace the advice of trained medical professionals. All matters regarding one's health require medical supervision. A physician should be consulted prior to adopting any program or programs described in this book. The author and publisher disclaim any liability arising directly or indirectly from the use of this book.

Copyright © 2007 by Jordan Rubin

Published in Nashville, Tennessee. Thomas Nelson is a trademark of Thomas Nelson, Inc.

Thomas Nelson Inc. titles may be purchased in bulk for educational, business, fundraising, or sales promotional use. For information, please e-mail SpecialMarkets@ThomasNelson.com.

Scripture quotations noted NKJV are taken from THE NEW KING JAMES VERSION®. © 1979, 1980, 1982, Thomas Nelson, Inc. Used by permission. All right reserved

Scripture quotations noted KJV are taken from THE KING JAMES VERSION.

Library of Congress Cataloging-in-Publication Data

Rubin, Jordan.
    The great physician's RX for high blood pressure / by Jordan Rubin, with Joseph Brasco.
    p. cm.
    Includes bibliographical references.
    ISBN 978-0-7852-1922-4
    1. Hypertension—Prevention—Popular works. 2. Hypertension—Religious aspects—Christianity. I. Brasco, Joseph. II. Title.
RC685.H8R777 2007
616.1'32061—dc22   2007014385

Printed in the United States of America

07 08 09 10 11 QW 5 4 3 2 1

CONTENTS

INTRODUCTION

Down for the Count

Back in elementary school, I was a huge Miami Dolphins fan who lived and died with the results of every Sunday afternoon football game. The following day in the schoolyard, my buddies and I would jabber about the exploits of our hero—golden-armed Dolphins quarterback Dan Marino. During his magical 1984 season, Marino threw for an NFL record forty-eight touchdowns (which Peyton Manning eclipsed in 2004) and 5,084 yards. "You were basically at Dan's mercy," said Ronnie Lott, the Hall of Fame defensive back.[1]

My Dolphins kept winning—they were 14-2 during the 1984 regular season—until they reached the ultimate game: Super Bowl XIX. Awaiting my favorite team were the San Francisco 49ers, led by legendary quarterback Joe Montana. Much of the Super Bowl hype focused on the passing battle between Marino and Montana, and I can still remember how excited I was—just a fourth grader—to attend my first Super Bowl party at a friend's house.

Unfortunately for Dan Marino and the Dolphins, Joe Montana dominated the gridiron that afternoon. Joe deftly moved the ball at will, completing twenty-four of thirty-five passes for a Super Bowl record 331 yards and three touchdowns as the 49ers cruised to the NFL championship, 38–16. Montana was named the Super Bowl MVP, and his exploits later prompted the town fathers of

Ismay, Montana, population twenty-two, to temporarily rename their city Joe, Montana.

I thought of Super Bowl XIX when I heard Joe Montana go public a couple of years ago with news that he was suffering from high blood pressure. It seems that during an annual check-up, Joe's doctor noticed elevated blood pressure levels. When she asked a few questions about his family history, the middle-aged football star revealed that his mother and two brothers had high blood pressure and his grandfather passed away at age fifty-four because of heart disease.

"When my doctor told me, 'If you don't get to see the cardiologist today, then try to stay away from any strenuous activities,' I knew that wasn't a good sign," Montana recalled.[2] Later, an MRI found that one of the arteries leading to his heart—the one called a "widow-maker"—was clogged like a drainpipe oozing with sludge.

In the game of life, Joe had been blindsided and sacked for a loss by high blood pressure, something that happens millions of times each year in this country. An estimated one in every three American adults—sixty-five million in all—has high blood pressure, according to the latest statistics from the Census Bureau and the National Health and Nutrition Examination Survey.[3] Even more disconcerting is that the number of US adults with high blood pressure has risen dramatically in the last decade, reversing a downward trend begun in the 1970s.

High blood pressure—also known as hypertension—increases your risk of developing cardiovascular disease and kidney disease, as well as having a stroke. The scary thing about high blood pressure is that there are no warning signs or symptoms for this condition, which is why it has been nicknamed the "silent killer." While anyone can develop high blood pressure, regardless of his or her race or gender, the risk for high blood pressure increases as one ages, and individuals with diabetes are especially susceptible. More men than women have hypertension until age fifty-five, when women start gaining on men and finally overtake them. Although there's a prevailing perception that high blood pressure is a "man's disease," the reality is that by age seventy-five, high blood pressure is more common among women than men.[4] ↙

The prevalence of high blood pressure in African-Americans is among the highest of all people groups. Also at risk are obese individuals, heavy drinkers, and women who take birth control pills. High blood pressure often runs in families—an estimated 30 to 60 percent of cases are inherited—so if your parents or close blood relatives have high blood pressure, you should have your blood pressure checked regularly.

In general, the older you are, the greater your chance of developing high blood pressure because the arteries naturally "harden" as people reach the middle-age years and beyond. Men seem to develop high blood pressure most often between the ages of thirty-five and fifty-five, and women are more likely to develop it after menopause, according to the American Heart Association.[5] Once high blood pressure develops, it usually lasts a lifetime unless steps are taken to control it. The good news is that high blood pressure can be curbed, and the Great Physician's prescription can be part of a successful treatment program.

A BASIC CHECK-UP

Many people don't understand what blood pressure is or why it's important. First of all, blood is carried from the heart to all parts of your body in vessels called *arteries*. Blood circulates through-out the body around the clock, feeding and oxygenating your cells, removing toxins, and defending your organs from disease and degeneration.

You need some sort of pressure inside the arteries to keep the blood moving, just as you need pressure in a garden hose to water your plants. Blood pressure is the force of the blood push-ing against the walls of the arteries. For those suffering from hypertension, this pressure is abnormally high and stays elevated over time.

Two basic things happen inside the body to cause high blood pressure:

1. The heart is pumping blood with excessive force.
2. The body's blood vessels have narrowed from the build-up of plaque or cholesterol, resulting in the blood flow exerting more pressure against the vessels' walls.

Each time the heart beats, which happens about sixty to seventy-five times a minute when you're at rest, it pumps out blood into the arteries. Your blood pressure is at its highest when the heart beats, pumping the blood. This is called *systolic pressure.* When the heart is at rest, or between beats, your blood pressure falls. This is called the *diastolic pressure.* For most of your waking hours, your blood pressure remains the same, except when you're exercising, of course.

Blood pressure is always given as a reading of these two numbers, the systolic and diastolic pressures, and both numbers mean something. When you're escorted to a doctor's examination room, a nurse or physician's assistant will usually take your blood pressure using a *sphygmomanometer*. This device includes a black cuff wrapped around the upper arm, a pump to inflate the cuff and stop the blood flow in your artery for a few seconds, and a valve to let the air out of the cuff and start blood flowing again.

A dial records the blood pressure reading. The first number read is for the systolic pressure, followed by a second number for the diastolic pressure. So when a nurse announces your blood pressure, she might say something like, "You're 110 over 70."

If you hear that pronouncement, that's good because the level you want to be is something in the neighborhood of 120/80 or less. When your blood pressure numbers push toward 140/90 or higher, eyebrows rise in the doctor's office, because that means you're an official candidate for high blood pressure. Your heart is working harder, your arteries are taking a beating, and your chances of having a deadly heart attack, a debilitating stroke, or significant kidney problems have dramatically increased.

It's All in the Numbers

Blood pressure, which is measured in millimeters of mercury, can be categorized as optimal, normal, high normal, and hypertensive. The hypertensive category can be broken down further, according to severity.

Two numbers are used to describe blood pressure: systolic pressure and diastolic pressure. The systolic pressure, which is always higher and listed first, measures the force that blood exerts on the arterial walls as the heart pumps blood through the body's cardiovascular system. The diastolic pressure, which is always lower and called out second, is the measurement of force as the heart relaxes to allow blood to flow back into its chambers.

A systolic blood pressure reading higher than 120 is viewed as an indicator of heart troubles down the road for middle-aged and older adults. A diastolic blood pressure reading higher than 80 is a predictor of heart attacks and strokes in young adults or people of any age suffering from hypertension.

Here are what blood pressure readings mean:

- Optimal blood pressure: anything below 120/80

- Normal blood pressure: 120/80 up to 130/85

- High normal blood pressure: 130/85 to 139/89

- Hypertension, or high blood pressure: 140/90

- Mild hypertension: 140/90 to 159/99

- Moderate hypertension: 160/100 to 179/109

- Severe hypertension: 180/110 to 209/119

- Very severe hypertension: anything over 210/120

A health care provider cannot make a correct diagnosis of high blood pressure just from the results of a single reading. If your blood pressure has measured 140/90 or higher on at least two separate occasions, your doctor may recommend a twenty-four-hour blood pressure monitor, which will show whether your blood pressure remains chronically high. This will help doctors decide whether you have hypertension.

According to the American Heart Association, the cause for high blood pressure is unknown in 90 to 95 percent of cases. The heart, brain, and kidneys can handle increased pressure for years without any symptoms or ill effects, until the fateful day when—bam!—your life is changed forever by a deadly heart attack or crippling stroke.

CONVENTIONAL TREATMENT

When Joe Montana learned that he had high blood pressure, he and his medical team huddled and came up with a game plan to care for the condition. His treatment regimen was fairly conservative, as you would expect for traditional medicine. He was directed to keep his right hand from gripping the salt shaker and to lay off salty foods, including his beloved potato chips. In addition, Joe, in his late forties, was given instructions to get back into the gym again and resume exercising. Joe's doctor also put him on a calcium channel blocker, a prescription drug that lowers one's blood pressure.

Physicians take high blood pressure seriously because they know that hypertension increases the risk for heart disease and stroke, the first- and third-leading causes of death among Americans. In addition, health care professionals understand that high blood pressure is like a red warning light on the dashboard of a car: something's not running right under the hood. If action is taken immediately, there's usually enough time to perform a few repairs before the engine overheats and blows a gasket.

Conventional treatment often involves the doctor sitting down with the patient—like Joe Montana—and discussing the importance of making lifestyle changes. For those with moderately high or severely high blood pressure readings, physicians will go a step further and urge their patients to begin taking antihypertension drugs.

Lifestyle recommendations revolve around two phrases:

1. No salt.
2. Start exercising.

The current recommendations from US government health professionals is that we should consume less than 2.4 grams of sodium per day, or the equivalent of one teaspoon of table salt daily. It comes as no surprise to me that Americans consume more salt than they need. Like horses that can't stop using a "salt lick," American appetites have been trained to crave salty snacks, and sodium is found in nearly all processed foods, including processed meats like breakfast sausage and hot dogs, as well as canned tuna, roast beef, and sliced turkey breast. Cheese, soups, condiments, sauces, and canned vegetables are all loaded with sodium.

I'll have a lot more to say about salt and sodium in my next chapter, "Key #1: Eat to Live," but for now, health professionals from traditional *and* alternative medicine agree that those with high blood pressure should adopt lower-sodium diets or eliminate salt altogether to keep their blood pressure rates under control.

If you happen to be overweight or obese, you will be urged to do something about those extra pounds. Being too heavy and having hypertension go hand in hand, but thin people are not off the hook. Interestingly, thin folks with hypertension are at *higher* risk for heart attacks and strokes than obese people with high blood pressure. If you're scratching your head, then you should know that health experts surmise that thin people with hypertension are more likely to have enlarged hearts or stiff arteries, which are primary causes of high blood pressure.[6]

The National Heart, Lung, and Blood Institute (NHLBI) has created categories to help doctors make basic treatment recommendations for people with high-normal or high blood pressure (see sidebar on page x). In addition, they rank patients in one of three groups (A, B, and C) according to their risk factors for heart disease.

Those in Risk Group A have no known risk factors for heart disease, and only women are in this group. Here is the recommended treatment protocol for those in Risk Group A:

- High normal blood pressure (130/85 to 139/89): lifestyle changes in diet and exercise

- Mild blood pressure (140/90 to 159/99): a yearlong trial of lifestyle changes

- Moderate blood pressure: (160/100 to 179/109): lifestyle changes and medications

- Severe blood pressure: (anything over 180/110): lifestyle changes and medications

Those in Risk Group B have at least one risk factor for heart disease but have no problems with organs such as their heart, kidneys, or eyes. Here is the recommended treatment protocol for those in Risk Group B:

- High normal blood pressure (130/85 to 139/89): lifestyle changes in diet and exercise
- Mild blood pressure (140/90 to 159/99): a six-month trial of lifestyle changes, but medications are considered for patients with multiple risk factors
- Moderate blood pressure: (160/100 to 179/109): lifestyle changes and medications
- Severe blood pressure: (anything over 180/110): lifestyle changes and medications

Those in Risk Group C have diabetes with or without problems with organs such as the heart, kidneys, or eyes. Here is the recommended treatment protocol for those in Risk Group C:

- High normal blood pressure (130/85 to 139/89): lifestyle changes and medications
- Mild blood pressure (140/90 to 159/99): lifestyle changes and medications

- Moderate blood pressure: (160/100 to 179/109): lifestyle changes and medications

- Severe blood pressure: (anything over 180/110): lifestyle changes and medications

When it comes to treating hypertension with drugs, doctors have a wide range to choose from, and some have found that two or more medications work better than one. Some of the common classes of drugs are these:

1. **Diuretics.** These so-called "water pills" prompt the kidneys to flush excess water and sodium from the body.

2. **Beta-blockers.** Beta-blockers reduce nerve impulses to the heart and blood vessels, which cues the heart to beat slower and with less force.

3. **ACE inhibitors.** ACE stands for angiotensin-converting enzyme, and ACE inhibitors prevent the formation of a hormone (angiotensin II) that causes the blood vessels to narrow.

4. **Angiotensin antagonists.** Angiotensin antagonists shield blood vessels from angiotensin II, which causes blood vessels to widen and blood pressure to go down.

5. **Calcium channel blockers (CCBs).** Joe Montana took CCBs to keep calcium from entering the muscle cells of his heart and blood vessels. These cause the blood vessels to relax.

6. **Alpha blockers.** Alpha blockers reduce nerve impulses to blood vessels, which allows blood to pass more easily, causing blood pressure to decrease.

7. **Alpha-beta blockers.** This drug slows the heartbeat so that less blood is pumped through the blood vessels, causing blood pressure to go down.

8. **Nervous system inhibitors.** This is another medication that relaxes blood vessels by controlling nerve impulses.

9. **Vasodilators.** Vasodilators directly open blood vessels by relaxing the muscle in the vessel walls.

From these drug classes, health care professionals have more than seven hundred antihypertension medications to choose from, but according to the Mayo Clinic Web site, certain prescription medications, over-the-counter drugs, supplements, and other substances can induce or worsen hypertension or interfere with the action of medications you're taking to lower your blood pressure. When a substance you take, or another medical condition, leads to high blood pressure, it's called secondary high blood pressure.[7]

More than two-thirds of the sixty-five million Americans with hypertension are taking at least one medication for their afflictions, more often two or three, according to a report from the Jersey Shore University Medical Center.[8] The most popular are diuretics like Diuril, Hygroton, and Esidrix; beta-blockers like Inderal, Tenormin, and Levatol; ACE inhibitors like Capoten, Vasotec, and Accupril; calcium-channel blockers like Cardizem, Norvasc, and Plendil;

angiotensin-receptor blockers like Cozaar, Atacand, and Micardis; and alpha blockers like Cardura and Minipress.

While effective in lowering blood pressure as well as the risk for heart attack and strokes, prescription drugs do come with common side effects: fatigue, depression, irritability, urinary incontinence, constipation, loss of sexual drive, breast swelling in men, and allergic reactions. Some experience vivid dreams and nightmares or memory loss. Other side effects include coldness in the extremities, asthma, and gastrointestinal problems.[9]

Another Take

Medications to combat high blood pressure are among the most widely prescribed drugs in the world—but they're not cheap, averaging forty to one hundred and fifty dollars a month. And many hypertension sufferers have to take two or more medications.

William Campbell Douglass, M.D., author of more than twenty books and editor of *Real Health*, a monthly alternative health newsletter (www.realhealthnews.com), had some sage insights into the connection between prescription drugs and hypertension. "I think that most doctors are forgetting—if they ever knew at all—that hypertension isn't a disease in itself," he wrote. "Hypertension is only a symptom of some other malfunction in your body. It's possible that the elevated blood pressure is a protective effect, enabling the heart to get blood to all the tissues in spite of the disease, whatever that might be. But since we still haven't figured out what that reason is, most physicians just throw drugs at the symptom and consider the problem solved when the high blood pressure goes down."

Dr. Douglass said that people taking hypertension medications inevitably feel worse on the drugs. "You would think this would signal to the doctor that he's making the patient worse . . . the problem here is that just because the drugs have made the hypertension go away, that doesn't mean you're 'cured'—or even safe, for that matter."[10]

With hundreds of high blood pressure medications available, consumers need to be aware of the pros and cons of taking them, which can be discussed with their doctors. Often, finding the correct dosage or combination that effectively lowers your blood pressure takes time, patience, and perseverance by both patient and doctor. "It may be annoying to take pills that possibly have side effects, especially if you felt fine before treatment," said the American Heart Association. "Don't be discouraged if you must be treated indefinitely. Some people can reduce their drug dosages after achieving normal blood pressure and maintaining it for a year or more. You usually can't stop treatment entirely. Coping with the inconvenience of medication is still much better than suffering a stroke or heart attack."[11]

ALTERNATIVE TREATMENTS

More and more of those with high blood pressure don't want to subject themselves to the myriad side effects that come from taking antihypertension drugs, nor do they believe that medications address the underlying causes of high blood pressure. Alternative medicine therapies stress ways to reduce stress through meditation, yoga, biofeedback, and even hypnosis. Proponents say if you feel your blood pressure rise while stuck in rush-hour traffic, then you can practice meditative breathing techniques and focus attention on your breath to calm your body—and your cardiovascular system. *Prescription for Natural Cures* suggests placing ten drops of Bach Flower extract under the tongue and holding the drops in place for thirty seconds before swallowing as a way to deal with feelings of panic and anger.

Traditional Chinese medicine teaches that hypertension is usually due to a lack of energy (*chi*) circulating in the body. Treatment centers use acupuncture to unblock and rebalance the flow of *chi* to restore health by inserting very thin needles at certain points of the body to produce a new "energy flow" along the body's meridians. Other types of acupuncture may use heat, pressure, or mild electrical current to provoke energy flow along these meridians.

Ayurvedic medicine, the traditional medicine of India, treats hypertension according to each person's metabolic type. Virender Sodhi, M.D. and director of the Ayurvedic and Naturopathic Clinic in Bellevue, Washington, believes that high blood pressure is most often found in *pitta* and *kapha* types, usually due to a combination of genetics and lifestyle. He puts his patients on a diet low in sodium, cholesterol, and triglycerides (the latter causing the blood to become viscous, which raises blood pressure levels).[12]

Dr. Sodhi also asks his patients to undertake yoga breathing exercises in an effort to relax the body and stimulate the cardio-vascular system. Breathing through one nostril and then the other, for ten to fifteen minutes at a time, is highly effective in lowering blood pressure. "I have patients try this in the office, and after ten minutes, their blood pressure drops considerably," he said.[13]

Ancient relaxation methods that include controlled breathing and gentle physical activity—such as yoga, Qigong, and Tai Chi—are beneficial. People with mild hypertension who prac-ticed these healing techniques daily for two to three months expe-rienced significant decreases in their blood pressure, had lower levels of stress hormones, and were less anxious compared with subjects in control groups, according to the Cleveland Clinic.[14]

Finally, for those seeking an alternative medicinal route, hawthorn is a heart tonic used in herbal medicine as a folk rem-edy. It is believed to decrease blood pressure, increase heart muscle contraction, increase blood flow to the heart muscle, and decrease the heart rate.

WHERE WE GO FROM HERE

Somehow, I don't see Joe Montana patiently breathing through one nostril for ten minutes while he waits for his blood pressure to drop. After learning that he had high blood pressure, the four-time Super Bowl winner started taking two medications to fight his high blood pressure: a calcium channel blocker and an

ACE inhibitor, which he said lowered his blood pressure to an optimal reading of 115 over 75.

Montana's difficulties with high blood pressure captured the media's attention, which prompted feature stories in dozens of newspapers and magazines. Novartis, a pharmaceutical company that produces high-blood-pressure medications, knew a celebrity endorser when they saw one, so they inked the "Comeback Kid" to promote the "Take the Pressure Off . . . with Better Blood Pressure Control" campaign to get the word out. (You can check Joe's story out at www.takethepressureoff.com.)

I have a different game plan for fighting high blood pressure, however, and I believe that following the 7 Keys that make up the Great Physician's prescription for health and wellness can set you down the right road toward lowering your high blood pressure and regaining your health. My strategy for defeating hypertension is based on seven keys to unlock your God-given health potential that I first described in my foundational book *The Great Physician's Rx for Health and Wellness.* Here are the 7 Keys:

- Key #1: Eat to live.

- Key #2: Supplement your diet with whole food nutritionals, living nutrients, and superfoods.

- Key #3: Practice advanced hygiene.

- Key #4: Condition your body with exercise and body therapies.

- Key #5: Reduce toxins in your environment.

- Key #6: Avoid deadly emotions.
- Key #7: Live a life of prayer and purpose.

A couple of these keys, I admit, may not seem to directly relate to hypertension, but they are part of living a healthy lifestyle. I'm confident the Great Physician's prescription can work for you because I've heard from plenty of folks about how the Great Physician's prescription is helping them live the life they've always dreamed of.

If you or a loved one has been medically diagnosed with high blood pressure, count yourself among the fortunate, since the vast majority of those with high blood pressure travel through life blissfully unaware that their hearts and their blood vessels are working harder than they should be. You have a chance to do something, and I urge you to pay close attention because I believe the Great Physician's prescription can get those high blood pressure readings moving in the right direction.

Better health won't happen overnight, but I believe you have a God-given health potential that is waiting to be unlocked with the right keys. I want to challenge you to incorporate these timeless principles and allow God to transform your health today.

KEY #1

Eat to Live

When football great Joe Montana learned he had high blood pressure, he joked that his kids employed a "zone defense" to keep him from reaching for the salt shaker at the family dinner table.

As mentioned in the Introduction, it'll take a lot more than hiding the salt shaker to lower your intake of sodium, which is the first thing doctors suggest when you have high blood pressure. The way I view things, anyone with hypertension who circles a buffet table before an afternoon NFL doubleheader should be gang-tackled because most snack foods—zesty tortilla chips, salted popcorn, wedges of imported cheese, or sliced wieners with toothpicks—contain high levels of sodium.

Sodium is a ubiquitous ingredient found in zillions of boxed, packaged, frozen, and bagged foods—such as pretzels and potato chips—but it's also hidden in many processed foods like ketchup and salad dressing. Even something sweet can have sodium: a grande Starbucks Java Chip Frappuccino contains 310 milligrams of sodium, and one Krispy Kreme Glazed Chocolate Cake doughnut has 310 milligrams, or around 15 percent of your daily allowance. It shouldn't surprise anyone that the average American eats two to three times the amount of salt that he or she should.

Pass the Herbamare, Please

If salty foods are an acquired taste, then this nation is hooked on salt. An estimated one-fourth of our sodium intake comes from salt added to a boiling pot of water or sprinkled on our food by restaurant cooks or those of us in the family kitchen. In addition, millions reach for a salt shaker each day and mindlessly douse their hot entrees with salt without tasting it first.

I never use regular table salt at home or away, to use a football term. When my food can use a little seasoning, I reach for a shaker of Herbamare, a flavorful blend of sea salt and fourteen organic herbs such as leek, cress, chive, parsley, garlic, and basil. A Swiss medical scientist named Alfred Vogel, M.D., developed Herbamare years ago.

If my wife, Nicki, is cooking up a storm—or if I have kitchen duty, since I enjoy cooking every now and then— we'll also use Celtic Sea Salt, RealSalt, or Himalayan Crystal Salt. These natural salts have nothing in common with table salt, which is 97.5 percent sodium chloride and 2.5 percent chemicals such as iodine and moisture absorbents.[1]

Regular table salt has been chemically cleaned in the production process and is not even in the same health league as "organic" salts that come from the ocean floor or pristine sources like the Himalayas. "Natural crystal salt does not contribute to high blood pressure like typical table salt," said my friend, Dr. Joe Mercola of Mercola.com, which is why Celtic Salt, Herbamare, and Himalayan Crystal Salt can be found in our home.

Reducing salt intake in your diet will be as difficult as evading a blitzing cornerback unless you adopt the first key of the Great Physician's prescription, which is "Eat to Live." This key places a heavy emphasis on doing two things:

1. Eating what God created for food.
2. Eating food in a form that is healthy for the body.

Following these two vital concepts will give you a great chance to emerge victorious in your quest to push down those high blood pressure levels and put you on the road toward living a healthy, vibrant life.

To successfully lower your intake of sodium, you will have to be intentional about what you eat from this day forward, especially if your diet is high in processed foods. That's where more than 80 percent of the sodium in most people's diets comes from.[2] I'm convinced that too many people coast through life without thinking longer than a TV timeout about the significance of what they're eating, which is why we're having a national problem with high blood pressure. Most folks blithely eat their favorite snacks and comfort foods, largely unaware that too much sodium—especially the "inorganic" kind—causes blood pressure to rise, which makes their hearts work progressively harder to pump enough blood to the body's tissues and organs.

Part of the blame can be laid at the feet of modern media, which often broadcasts—especially during football games—alluring and effective commercials for a variety of high-sodium foods, including deep-dish, stuffed-crust, double-cheese Italian sausage pizza, for example. Before you know it, you're calling Domino's during halftime and asking them to deliver a large hand-tossed MeatZZa Feast pizza to your front door. Just two slices—or one-fourth of a large pizza—contains 1,620 milligrams of sodium, or 70 percent of the recommended daily amount.

The American Heart Association recommends that most people limit their daily sodium intake to 2,300 milligrams per day. That's tough to follow since the standard American diet—boxed cereal or ham and eggs in the morning, cheeseburger and salty fries for lunch, and a take-out pepperoni pizza and toasted garlic bread for dinner—contains way too much sodium, something in the order of 4,000 to 6,000 milligrams a day.

Read the Food Labels Closely

The US Food and Drug Administration has developed these definitions that appear on food packages to assist consumers watching their sodium intake:

- "low sodium" means the food has 140 milligrams or less of sodium per serving

- "very low sodium" means the food has 35 milligrams or less of sodium per serving

- "salt-free" means the food has 5 milligrams or less of sodium per serving

- "light in sodium" means the food has at least 50 percent less sodium than the original version of the food

- "reduced sodium" means the food has at least 25 percent less sodium than the original version of the product

SOME BETTER CHOICES

Salt is not Public Enemy #1. We need salt in the human diet for balanced bodily fluids and efficient muscle nerve function. The problem is we're getting too much salt from too many processed, frozen, or fast foods.

When it comes to lowering your intake of sodium, I don't think you can go wrong by eating any of the following foods on this comprehensive list compiled by my friend Rex Russell, M.D., in his book *What the Bible Says About Healthy Living.* I'm reprinting them here, along with the scriptural references, because many people aren't aware that the Bible is an excellent source of information about good nutrition and healthy living.

As you scan through this list, ask yourself if these are foods that you regularly eat:

- almonds (Gen. 43:11)
- barley (Judg. 7:13)
- beans (Ezek. 4:9)
- bread (1 Sam. 17:17)
- broth (Judg. 6:19)
- cakes (2 Sam. 13:8, and probably not the kind with frosting)
- cheese (Job 10:10)
- cucumbers, onions, leeks, melons, and garlic (Num. 11:5)
- curds of cow's milk (Deut. 32:14)
- figs (Num. 13:23)
- fish (Matt. 7:10)
- fowl (1 Kings 4:23)
- fruit (2 Sam. 16:2)
- game (Gen. 25:28)
- goat's milk (Prov. 27:27)
- grain (Ruth 2:14)
- grapes (Deut. 23:24)
- grasshoppers, locusts, and crickets (Lev. 11:22)
- herbs (Exod. 12:8)
- honey (Isa. 7:15) and wild honey (Ps. 19:10)
- lentils (Gen. 25:34)
- meal (Matt. 13:33 KJV)

- pistachio nuts (Gen. 43:11)
- oil (Prov. 21:17)
- olives (Deut. 28:40)
- pomegranates (Num. 13:23)
- quail (Num. 11:32)
- raisins (2 Sam. 16:1)
- salt (Job 6:6)
- sheep (Deut. 14:4)
- sheep's milk (Deut. 32:14)
- spices (Gen. 43:11)
- veal (Gen. 18:7-8)
- vegetables (Prov. 15:17)
- vinegar (Num. 6:3)[3]

When eaten in their natural forms and without processing, these foods that God created are naturally low in sodium and high in fiber. Many are also high in potassium, which is an important distinction for those with high blood pressure. While excessive consumption of dietary sodium is the main culprit of high blood pressure, numerous studies have shown that those with hypertension are also deficient in their intake of potassium, an electrolyte (or mineral salt) that's important to the human nervous system and heart, kidney, and adrenal functions. Insufficient potassium can exaggerate the effects of sodium, and the first sign of a potassium deficiency is a general feeling of malaise, or weakness.

If you eat plenty of fresh fruits and vegetables—like the ones described by Dr. Russell—you'll most likely have sufficient potassium in your diet. The Duke University Medical Center and the American Kidney Foundation recommend the following high potassium foods when fighting high blood pressure:

- all meats, especially poultry and fish
- apricots
- bananas
- cantaloupe
- honeydew melon
- kiwi
- lima beans
- milk
- oranges and orange juice
- potatoes (not fried, of course)
- prunes
- spinach
- tomatoes
- vegetable juice
- winter squash[4]

A different dietary approach is more favored by doctors, though. It's called the DASH Eating Plan—DASH, standing for Dietary Approaches to Stop Hypertension—and it was formulated after two studies conducted by scientists working for the National Heart, Lung, and Blood Institute (NHLBI) established a clear link between diet and the development of high blood pressure. The DASH Eating Plan is low in saturated fat, cholesterol, and total fat. The diet emphasizes fruits, vegetables, and low-fat dairy products and also includes whole grain products, fish, poultry, and nuts, while reducing the consumption of red meat, sweets, and sugar-containing beverages. The DASH plan is based on a person eating 2,000 calories a day.

As an example, the DASH diet recommends eating an eight-ounce steak while upping the consumption of fruits and vegetables instead of digging into a sixteen-ounce steak topped with fried onion rings. Instead of apple pie à la mode, you enjoy a fresh fruit medley.

While I'm all for a commonsense diet calling for plenty of servings of fruits, vegetables, whole grain products, and fish and poultry, the Great Physician's prescription for eating has some key differences. When I talk about consuming foods that God created in a form that is healthy for the body, I'm talking about choosing foods as close to the natural source as possible, which will give your body excellent sustenance, keep your blood pressure numbers in check, and give you the healthiest life possible. As you can probably figure out by now, I'm a proponent of natural foods grown organically since these are foods that God created in a form healthy for the body.

Under the DASH Eating Plan, those suffering from high blood pressure are counseled to choose lean meats and low-fat dairy products and to limit their intake of added fat to one food per meal. For instance, they could put a dab of margarine in their baked potato or slice of bread or add dressing to their salad, but they couldn't do all three things.

First of all, margarine is a no-no since it contains gobs of hydrogenated oils. In addition, certain "high fat" foods—steak, eggs, butter, and full-fat dairy products, when consumed from free-range and organic sources—contain fats that your body needs for optimal health. God, in His infinite wisdom, created certain fats to serve the following functions: play a vital role in bone health, enhance the immune system, protect the liver from alcohol and other toxins, and guard against harmful micro-organisms in the digestive tract.

The best examples of "good fats" are healthy saturated fats, omega-3 polyunsaturated fats, and monounsaturated (omega-9) fatty acids. You can find these fats in a wide range of foods: salmon, lamb, and goat meat; grass-fed cow's, goat's, and sheep's milk and cheese; coconuts, walnuts, olives, almonds, and avocados. These fats provide us with a concentrated source of energy and are the source material for cell membranes and various hormones.

The problem with the standard American diet is that people eat too many of the wrong foods containing the wrong fats and not enough of the right foods with the right fats. Two of the top fats and oils on my list are extra virgin coconut and olive oils, which are beneficial to the body and aid metabolism. I urge you to cook with extra virgin coconut oil, which is an extremely healthy food that few people have ever heard of.

A LOOK AT PROTEINS AND CARBOHYDRATES

Along with fats, two other macronutrients are important when you "Eat to Live." Proteins, which are one of the basic components of foods, are the essential building blocks of the body and involved in the function of every living cell. One of protein's main tasks is to provide specific nutrient material to grow and repair cells—especially in the body's arterial vessels.

All proteins are combinations of twenty-two amino acids, but your body cannot produce all twenty-two amino acids that you need in order to live a robust life. Scientists have discovered that eight essential amino acids are missing, meaning that they must come from sources outside the body. I know the following fact drives vegetarians and vegans crazy, but animal protein—chicken, beef, lamb, dairy, eggs, etc.—is the *only* complete protein source providing the Big Eight amino acids in the right quantities and ratios.

The conventional wisdom in the medical community is that animal protein contains large quantities of fat, which aggravates hypertension. Saturated fat is said to increase the level of low-density lipoproteins (LDL), which can stick to the side of the arterial walls and cause high blood pressure. Consuming less red meat is often promoted as a strong first step to getting high blood pressure under control.

While we could all stand to eat less low-quality, poorly raised, and chemical-laden red meat, the best approach to keep high blood pressure in check is to consume the leanest, healthiest sources of animal protein available, which come from organically raised cattle, sheep, goats, buffalo, and venison—animals that graze on pastureland grasses. Lean, grass-fed beef contains less saturated fat and less pro-inflammatory omega-6 fatty acids than conventionally grown grain-fed beef.

I'm confident that those battling hypertension have been eating the *wrong* kinds of meat for many years. For instance, hamburger is a high-fat meat found in every main dish from backyard burgers to spaghetti and meatballs, but in this country, the vast majority of hamburger is comprised of ground chuck with added fat from hormone-injected cattle eating pesticide-sprayed feed laced with antibiotics.

You would be much better off eating hamburger—as well as other cuts of beef—produced from range-fed and pasture-fed cows. Natural beef is much healthier for you than assembly-line "production" cuts filling our nation's supermarket meat cases. Grass-fed beef is leaner and lower in calories than grain-fed beef, and the flavor is tremendous. Grass-fed beef is higher in heart-friendly omega-3 fatty acids and important vitamins like vitamins B_{12} and E. When eaten in moderation, I don't believe lean red meats will exacerbate hypertension.

For those seeking to reduce their consumption of red meat, consider eating "free-range" chicken and fish captured from lakes, streambeds, or ocean depths. Fish with scales and fins caught in the wild are excellent sources of protein, as well as healthy fats, vitamins, and minerals, and they provide all the essential amino acids.

Wild fish, which is nutritionally far superior to farm-raised, should be consumed liberally by those with high blood pressure.

These so-called "oily" fish are particularly beneficial because they contain high levels of omega-3 fatty acids, which keep the heart and blood vessels in good condition. Eating wild-caught fish can lower levels of other fats in the blood, which reduces problems caused by hardening of the arteries or high blood pressure.

You should shop for fish with scales and fins such as halibut, tuna, tilapia, and trout, and stay away from fish without both scales and fins, such as catfish, shark, and swordfish. Shop for fish caught in the wild from oceans and rivers and not "feedlot salmon" raised on fish farms, which don't compare to their cold-water cousins in terms of taste or nutritional value. While it's great to see more people eating the tender pink meat of farm-raised Atlantic salmon, it's never going to nutritionally match what comes from the wild. The salmon from fish farms spend several years lazily circling concrete tanks, fattening up on pellets of salmon chow, not streaking through the ocean eating small marine life as they're supposed to.

The better alternative is to purchase fresh salmon and other fish from your local fish market or health-food store. Look for the labels "Alaskan" or "wild-caught." Wild-caught fish is an absolutely incredible food and should be consumed liberally. Supermarkets and health-food stores are stocking these types of foods in greater quantities these days, and of course, they are found in natural-food stores, fish markets, and specialty stores.

Besides fats and proteins, the third macronutrient contained in food is carbohydrates, which, by definition, are the sugars and starches contained in plant foods. Sugars and starches, like fats, are not inherently bad for you. The problem is that the standard

American diet includes way too many foods containing these carbohydrates—foods brimming with sodium. Sugar and its sweet relatives—high fructose corn syrup, sucrose, molasses, and maple syrup—are among the first ingredients listed in staples such as cereals, breads, buns, pastries, doughnuts, cookies, ketchup, and ice cream. And as I said before, many of these processed foods contain surprisingly high amounts of sodium.

Restricting the consumption of carbohydrates and wisely choosing your carbs should result in an improvement of your high blood pressure. The carbohydrates you want to consume are low glycemic, high nutrient, and low sugar. These would be most high-fiber fruits (especially berries), vegetables, nuts, seeds, and some legumes, plus a small amount of whole grain products (sprouted, soaked, or sour-leavened), which are always better than refined carbohydrates that have been stripped of their vital fiber, essential fatty acids, vitamins, and mineral components.

You're probably aware that many people battling high blood pressure are also battling the bulge around their midsection. You don't have to be related to Albert Einstein to understand that being overweight increases your risk of developing hypertension. Medical professionals agree that losing even ten pounds can lower blood pressure and other risk factors for heart disease.

If you know—or have been told by your doctor—that you need to lose weight so that your blood pressure can come down, please know that I don't recommend any of the popular "low-carb" diets like Atkins, South Beach, or The Zone. This trio of popular diets differ in the details, but generally speaking they call for an increase in high-protein sources such as meat, fish, and dairy and a reduction in the intake of carbohydrates like bread, pasta, and rice, which causes the body to burn excess body fat for fuel.

Low-carb eating has had quite a following in the last few years. The low-carb craze peaked in early 2004 when over 9 percent of US adults claimed to be on a low-carb diet, according to market research firm NPD Group. That figure, however, declined to 2.2 percent a little more than a year later, the same time Atkins Nutritionals, the company distributing Atkins products, announced that it was seeking bankruptcy protection.[5]

It doesn't surprise me that the low-carb boom fizzled since the only good thing about low-carb diets was that people avoided excess sugar and white flour. Despite the fact that each of the aforementioned diets has some good recommendations, my biggest beef with low-carb diets is that most of these health plans advocate a high consumption of meat products that the Bible calls detestable, allow only limited amounts of nutrient-rich fruits and vegetables, and encourage the consumption of artificial sweeteners and preservatives. Replacing processed foods with natural and organic foods and consuming carbohydrates such as fruits, vegetables, nuts, seeds, legumes, and cultured dairy products is a much better way to lose weight and lower your blood pressure. I believe you get there quicker by eating the healthiest, most nutritious food possible right away.

TOP HEALING FOODS

Following a diagnosis of high blood pressure, most doctors and nurses will stress the importance of eating fruits, vegetables, whole grain breads and cereals, moderate amounts of meat and dairy products, and cutting back on sugar and fats.

While I concur with much of what conventional medicine recommends for those with high blood pressure regarding their nutrition, I want to make some additional points about what you should be eating since this is a key part of *The Great Physician's Rx for High Blood Pressure*. I've come up with a list of Top Healing Foods that should find a way into your pantry or refrigerator—today.

Just as a diet heavy in restaurant meals and snack foods is a primary cause of high blood pressure, making changes in your diet is a great way to fight it. I've been talking in general terms about nutritional recommendations, but now let's take a closer look at what you should and shouldn't be eating when it comes to keeping hypertension in check and preventing heart attacks and strokes:

1. Healthy animal foods. I've already made a strong case for eating meat from organically raised grass-fed cattle, sheep, goats, buffalo, and venison that graze on nature's bountiful grasses as well as fish caught in the wild. For those with high blood pressure, the healthiest meat is fish caught in the wild, including salmon, sardines, herring, mackerel, tuna, snapper, bass, and cod. Wild-caught fish are a rich source of omega-3 fatty acids, which are also good for heart health.

One of the first associations between omega-3 fatty acids and human health was made in the 1970s when scientists studying the Inuit people of Greenland discovered that Inuits suffered far less coronary heart disease than Europeans, even though their diet was off-the-chart high in fat from eating whale and seal—including their blubber—as well as copious amounts of salmon.[6]

Just as there are meats you should eat for cardiovascular health, there are certain meats you must avoid. I'm talking about breakfast links, bacon, lunch meats, ham, hot dogs, bratwurst, and other sausages. In all of my previous books, I've consistently pointed out that pork—America's "other white meat"—should be avoided because pigs were called "unclean" in Leviticus and Exodus. God created pigs as scavengers—animals that survive just fine on any farm slop or water swill tossed their way. Pigs have a simple stomach arrangement: whatever a pig eats goes down the hatch, straight into the stomach, and out the back door in four hours max. They'll even eat their own excrement, if hungry enough.

Even if you decide to keep eating commercial beef instead of the organic version, I absolutely urge you to stop eating pork. Read Leviticus 11 and Deuteronomy 14 to learn what God said about eating clean versus unclean animals, where Hebrew words used to describe unclean meats can be translated as "detestable," "foul," and "putrid," the same terms the Bible uses to describe child sacrifice and even human waste.

Please realize that not all sea life is healthy to eat either. Shellfish and fish without fins and scales, such as catfish, shark, and eel, are also described in Leviticus 11 and Deuteronomy 14 as "unclean meats." God called hard-shelled crustaceans such as lobster, crabs, shrimp, and clams unclean because they are "bottom feeders," content to sustain themselves on excrement from other fish. To be sure, this purifies water but does nothing for the health of their flesh—or yours, if you eat them.

Eating detestable animal products fouls the body and may

lead to increases in heart disease and cancer by introducing toxins into the bloodstream. God declared these meats detestable and unclean because He understands the ramifications of eating them, and you should as well.

2. Cultured dairy products from goats, cows, and sheep. Medical doctors lump the saturated fats in dairy products in the same category as red meat, implicating fat intake as one of the key factors behind high blood pressure and cardiovascular disease. Thus, doctors recommend that we should not eat full-fat dairy products. When reaching for a half gallon of milk at the supermarket, they say, be sure to choose a low-fat version like 2 percent or skim milk.

I don't see things the same way because I have never heard of a cow, sheep, or goat producing 2 percent or skim milk. Reduced fat milk is less nutritious, less digestible, and can cause allergies. When it comes to keeping blood pressure levels in check, I recommend that you purchase dairy products derived from goat's milk and sheep's milk, or cultured dairy from grass-fed cows.

Another reason I prefer sheep's milk, goat's milk, and their cheeses lies in the milk's structure: its fat and protein molecules are tiny in size, which allows for rapid absorption in the digestive tract. Milk fat from healthy milk (organic, grass-fed) also contains a number of bioactive components, including conjugated linoleic acid (CLA). "Conjugated linoleic acid has been shown to possess activities that prevent cancer and the formation of cholesterol-containing plaques that contribute to heart disease [and high cholesterol]," said Michael Murray, author of *The Encyclopedia of Healing Foods.*[7]

Sheep's and goat's milk are less allergenic because they do not contain the same complex proteins found in cow's milk. I also recommend you consume milk in its cultured or fermented form, such as yogurt and kefir. The fermentation process makes the milk easier to digest, and its nutrients are more usable by the body. Cultured or fermented dairy products contain beneficial microorganisms or probiotics that help maintain healthy cholesterol levels and even lower elevated levels.

Finally, let me address one more food that directly relates to high blood pressure but maybe not the way you think it does—eggs. When someone is clinically diagnosed with hypertension, one of the first items they're told to strike off their grocery list is eggs because they have been associated with a greater risk of high blood pressure.

However, in research published in the *American Journal of Clinical Nutrition,* researchers at the University of Minnesota studied 4,304 men and women aged eighteen to thirty from various racial backgrounds and found that eating eggs one to three times a week was associated with an 11 to 21 percent *decrease* in hypertension risk. A correlating decrease was found for those eating dairy foods as well. University of Minnesota researchers believed that the rich variety of nutrients in eggs and dairy foods—phytonutrients, fiber, magnesium, potassium, and calcium—were the likely reason that these foods were good for those with hypertension.[8]

That news makes sense to me because organic high omega-3 eggs and dairy products are wonderful foods deserving Hall-of-Fame status. Take the humble egg, for example: this nutrient-dense food packs six grams of protein, a bit of vitamin B_{12}, vitamin E, lutein, riboflavin, folic acid, calcium, zinc, iron, and essential fatty acids into a mere seventy-five calories. I strongly urge you to buy high omega-3 eggs, which have become much more available in response to consumer demand. Natural food markets stock them, of course, but you'll find omega-3 eggs at major supermarket chains as well as warehouse clubs like Costco.

Finally, I urge you not to overlook cultured dairy products such as yogurt and kefir, which provide an excellent source of easily digestible protein, B vitamins, calcium, and probiotics.

3. A wide selection of fruits and vegetables. Everyone involved with high blood pressure, from the top medical specialists to those promoting natural cures, sings from the same song sheet: you need to increase your fruit and veggie consumption to prevent or battle hypertension since these foods are high in potassium. Yet the average American consumes far less than the recommended five to nine servings of fruits and vegetables daily, which is a shame. "Some people go through the whole day without eating a single vegetable," said Carolyn Katzin, a nutrition expert at UCLA and a spokeswoman for the American Cancer Society.[9]

A US government panel led by Lawrence Appel of Johns Hopkins University said that people need 4.7 grams of potassium a day to ward off high blood pressure. To achieve that, most Americans would have to eat about *ten* servings of fruits and vegetables a day.[10]

I'll settle for something between five and ten servings (although I will often consume ten to fifteen servings on any given day), which means that instead of reaching for a Danish for a midmorning snack or a candy bar in the afternoon, I bite into a banana or a handful of apricots. I recommend purchasing organic fruits and veggies, which are loaded with heart-healthy vitamins, minerals, fiber, and antioxidants. Shopping for organically grown fruits and veggies is easier these days since major supermarket chains—even Wal-Mart—are stocking more and more organic fruits and vegetables in their produce departments. Sure, you'll pay anywhere from 10 percent to 100 percent more, but what kind of price tag can you put on alleviating high blood pressure symptoms?

4. Soaked and sprouted seeds and grains. Like fruits and vegetables, whole grains, seeds, nuts, and breads made with sprouted or sour-leavened grains are blood-pressure-friendly foods. Apparently the fiber, vitamins, phytochemicals, and antioxidants in properly prepared whole grains—wheat, spelt, kamut, quinoa, amaranth, millet, buckwheat, barley, corn, oats, and rice—appear to work together in the fight against hypertension. "Whole grain" means the bran and germ are left on the grain during processing. "Soaked and sprouted grains" retain their plant enzymes when they are not cooked and are more digestible when cooked or baked.

5. Cultured and fermented vegetables. Often greeted with upturned noses at the dinner table, fermented vegetables, such as sauerkraut, pickled carrots, beets, or cucumbers, are brimming with vitamins, such as vitamin C, and contain almost four times the nutrients as unfermented cabbage.

The Japanese, who enjoy the second-longest lifespan in the world and lower rates of heart disease than their counterparts in the USA, eat fermented vegetables, from pickled cabbage to eggplant to daikon radish, with all their traditional meals.

6. Nuts and seeds. Most people, when they shop for nuts at the supermarket, pull a jar of peanuts off the shelves, which are coated with enough salt to stock a margarita bar.

You shouldn't purchase nuts sprayed with sodium and other artificial flavorings. Instead, you should purchase raw nuts (dry roasted is okay too) as well as seeds, which are protective to the heart. The Food and Drug Administration announced in 2003 that "scientific evidence suggests but does not prove that eating 1.5 ounces per day of most nuts, as part of a diet low in saturated fat and cholesterol, may reduce the risk of heart disease."[11]

I counted five qualifiers in that sentence, so the FDA wasn't treading too far out on a limb. But I've read plenty of research, including a Penn State study, showing that eating almonds, Brazil nuts, cashews, hazelnuts, macadamia nuts, pecans, pistachios, walnuts, sunflower seeds, and even lowly peanuts has a strong protective effect against coronary disease.

Try to eat some nuts or seeds daily. Grabbing a handful of almonds and cashews, which are excellent sources of magnesium, is a fine way to start you down the road toward better health.

7. Herbs and spices. One of the first things that those with high blood pressure hear from their doctors is that they have to clear away the table salt and other prepared seasonings that are major sources of sodium. Sodium causes the body to hold onto fluids, which causes the heart to work harder as it pumps the added fluids inside the body.

But don't think you're resigned to eating bland, unsavory foods the rest of your life. There's an exciting world of herbs and spices out there waiting to be discovered by you. I mentioned my personal favorite—a product called Herbamare—as well as "natural" salts like Celtic Sea Salt and RealSalt.

After tossing your salt shaker in the trash, treat your taste buds to a vast array of healthy spices that you can employ while cooking or barbecuing. Variety is the spice of life and waiting to be discovered. Squeezing a lemon on fish or meat has been done for centuries. Sautéing vegetables in coconut oil or organic butter can bring out their flavor. Sprinkling bay leaf, celery seeds, clove, coriander, cumin, dill weed, fennel, marjoram, mustard seed, nutmeg, oregano, paprika, peppercorn, saffron, sesame, and thyme on your food can open your palate to a brand new starburst of flavors.

Two household spices in your cupboard may have heart-healthy properties. Ginger, the world's most widely cultivated spice, contains natural chemicals that discourage blood clotting, lower cholesterol, and increases the force or strength of heart-muscle tissue. "Ginger offers a profound antioxidant principal action and observed effects, which include strengthening of the cardiac muscle and lowering of serum cholesterol," wrote Paul Schulick in *Ginger: Common Spice & Wonder Drug.*[12]

There's another household spice that you should look for ways to use, but you won't be able to spoon this one into your mouth. I'm talking about cayenne pepper, which is rich in organic calcium and potassium, making it good for those with high blood pressure. Cayenne pepper also contains a high amount of beta-carotene, an antioxidant that lowers bad LDL cholesterol levels.

8. Fruit and vegetable juices. Just as the increased consumption of fruits and vegetables is important in the fight to lower blood pressure, drinking fresh-squeezed fruit juice or raw vegetable juice made from a juicer can be extremely beneficial.

One "juice" that should be severely curtailed or stricken from your diet entirely is wine—as well as other alcoholic drinks. For some but not all people, alcohol causes blood pressure to rise, according to the National Heart, Lung, and Blood Institute. Alcoholic drinks also contain calories, which matters if you need to lose weight. Either way, the smart route would be the cessation of drinking wine, beer, or hard spirits until your blood pressure is back to normal levels.

9. Water. Water isn't a food, of course, but this calorie-free and sugar-free substance performs many vital tasks for the body: regulating the body temperature, carrying nutrients and oxygen to the cells, cushioning joints, protecting organs and tissues, and removing toxins. Water provides the viscosity in blood and plasma, almost like the lubricating effects of oil in a high-powered engine. Water helps move nutrients to your cells and helps keep cholesterol levels down. Not drinking enough water is bad for your body and for your blood pressure.

F. Batmanghelidj, M.D., and author of *Your Body's Many Cries for Water*, contends that high blood pressure is a signal from the body that it's not getting enough water. "In my scientific opinion, the most common and frequent reason [for high blood pressure] is a gradually establishing dehydration in the body."[13]

The way Dr. Batmanghelidj explains it, when the body is lacking water, it attempts to hold on to the available water supplies by resorting to vascular constriction throughout the body. This helps reduce the loss of water through the skin and through respiration, thus conserving the remaining water in the body. The result is a generalized drought and lack of water to fill all the blood vessels that facilitate the normal diffusion of water into vital cells. He adds that treating the symptoms of high blood pressure with diuretics will further dehydrate the body and could lead to blockage of the arteries leading to the heart and brain.

The answer is in drinking a minimum of eight glasses of water a day to stay hydrated. Drinking plenty of water is not only healthy for the body, but it may save your life. Sure, you'll go to the bathroom more often, but is that so bad? Drinking plenty of water is a key part of the Great Physician's Rx for High Blood Pressure Battle Plan (see page 75), so keep a water bottle close by and drink water before, during, and between meals.

I take hydration seriously even though I don't have high blood pressure. I set a forty-eight-ounce bottle of water on my office desk as a reminder to keep putting fluids into my system. My record for drinking water is one and one-quarter gallons of water in a day during a fast, but I won't reveal how many trips I made to the bathroom that day!

Okay, so you'll treble your steps to the lavatory by consciously drinking more water, but you'll be giving your cardiovascular system the "lubrication" it needs to keep everything moving . . . rather than backing up and causing high blood pressure.

10. Coconut water. If you really want to step up your hydration efforts, then make the effort to try drinking coconut water, which is one of the world's richest sources of potassium. Coconut water is the thin liquid found inside Thai or young coconuts, where coconut milk is made from steeping the coconut and scraping out the meat, adding just enough water to form a thick, milky substance.

It's been said that there is no water as pure as coconut water, which contains a variety of minerals and other nutrients. You can usually find Thai or young coconuts at local health food stores, and I'm sure the staff will be glad to show you how to crack a coconut and extract its water. For the less adventurous, there are a few brands of packaged coconut water available for purchase.

11. Apple cider vinegar. As you can tell, *The Great Physician's Rx for High Blood Pressure* calls for drinking a lot of healthy liquids, and apple cider vinegar deserves a place at the table.

Apple cider vinegar is made from the squeezed liquid of crushed apples. Sugar and yeast are added to the liquid to start the fermentation process, which turns the sugar into alcohol. During a second round of fermentation, the alcohol is converted by acetic acid-forming bacteria into vinegar. The acetic acid is what gives vinegar its sour taste, as well as its minerals: potassium, phosphorus, calcium, magnesium, natural silicon, pectin, malic acid, and tartaric acids. Apple cider vinegar helps the body rebalance its acid level, and its icky taste hasn't stopped aficionados from singing the praises of apple cider vinegar, or ACV for short.

The "Johnny Appleseed" of apple cider vinegar is Vermont physician D.C. Jarvis, M.D., who injected the lore of folk medicine into his practice. His book *Folk Medicine* has sold over three million copies during the last fifty years. For patients with high blood pressure who visited his practice, Dr. Jarvis counseled the daily intake of two teaspoons of apple cider vinegar mixed with two teaspoons of raw honey in a glass of warm water.

Remember: don't drink apple cider vinegar unless it is well diluted. I recommend two teaspoons of ACV and two teaspoons of honey mixed in eight to twelve ounces of warm water; otherwise, you'll be puckering your lips and shaking your head at the tartness of the first sip.

Practice Fasting Once a Week

I'm a firm believer in the value of giving the body time off from the round-the-clock digestive cycle, which will also give your heart less work to do and potentially lower your blood pressure. Fasting can be a potent, natural therapy to lower blood pressure.

I think it's best—and realistic—to concentrate on completing a one-day partial fast once a week. Fasting is a form of discipline that isn't easy for someone who's never done it. If you've never voluntarily fasted for a day, I urge you to try it—preferably toward the end of the week. I've found that Thursdays or Fridays work best for me because the week is winding down and the weekend is coming up. For instance, I won't eat breakfast and lunch so that when I break my fast and eat dinner that night, my body has gone between eighteen and twenty hours without food or sustenance since I last ate dinner the night before.

The benefits are immediate: you'll feel great, lose weight, look younger, save money, save time, and become closer to the Lord. Fasting is a means of denying the flesh because the stomach and the brain work overtime in reminding you "Hey! I'm hungry!" That's why they call it the "fasting headache." When you fast and pray (two words that seem to go hand in hand in Scripture), you are pursuing God in your life and opening yourself to experiencing a renewed sense of well-being and dependence upon the Lord.

WHAT NOT TO EAT

When you're dealing with high blood pressure, there are a number of foods that should never find a way onto your plate or into your hands. I call them "The Dirty Dozen." Some I've already discussed elsewhere in this chapter, while the rest are presented for the first time here with a short commentary:

1. Processed meat and pork products. These meats top my list because they are staples in the standard American diet and extremely unhealthy because of the high amounts of sodium they contain.

The meats you should steer clear of are breakfast links, bacon, lunch meats, ham, bratwurst, and other sausages. These foods introduce pathogenic organisms and toxins into the bloodstream, and God called them "detestable" and "unclean" in Leviticus and Exodus. These processed meats also contain additives like nitrates that were introduced during the curing process. Nitrates can convert into nitrite, which can turn into nitrosamines, a powerful cancer-causing chemical.

2. Shellfish and fish without fins and scales, such as catfish, shark, and eel. Am I saying *au revoir*, *sayonara*, and *adios* to lobster thermidor, shrimp tempura, and carnitas burritos? That's what I'm saying.

3. Hydrogenated oils. Hydrogenated fats and partially hydrogenated fats are found in practically every processed food, from Dunkin' Donuts to Wonder Bread, from Ding Dongs to Dove Bars. Most of the oils used in households today—soybean, safflower, cottonseed, and corn—are partially hydrogenated oils, which, by definition, are liquid fats that have been injected with hydrogen gas at high temperatures under high pressure to make them solid at room temperature.

Hydrogenation increases shelf life and gives flavor stability to foods, but it also produces unsaturated trans-fatty acids, also known as trans fats. Mark my words: trans fats are terribly unhealthy for the body and do nothing positive for your blood pressure. For years, you couldn't find out how much trans fat was in the food you were eating. That changed in 2006 with the introduction of new Nutrition Facts labels stating the amount of trans fat in a particular food. I welcome this long-overdue change in food labeling, although I don't see the sales of processed foods declining.

Be aware that the hydrogenated or partially hydrogenated fats in processed foods—from commercial cakes, pastries, and desserts to just about every wrapped-in-plastic item sold in a neighborhood convenience store—are bad for heart health. If you can hop off the junk food bandwagon and leave all those hydrogenated oils behind, your heart will thank you.

4. Artificial sweeteners. The DASH Eating Plan says you can use artificial sweeteners to help satisfy your sweet tooth while sparing the sugar. I completely disagree with this government recommendation. Aspartame (found in NutraSweet and Equal), saccharine (Sweet'N Low), and sucralose (Splenda), which are chemicals several hundred times sweeter than sugar, should be completely avoided. Simply put, these are not foods at all, but combinations of artificial chemicals that may lead to serious problems for those who consume them.

5. White flour. White flour isn't a problematic chemical like artificial sweeteners, but it's virtually worthless and not healthy for you because of the processing that goes into turning wheat into white flour.

After wheat is harvested, the wheat stalks are trucked to flour mills and rinsed with various chemical bleaches that sound like items on a vocabulary test from a high school biology class: nitrogen oxide, chlorine, chloride, nitrosyl, and benzoyl peroxide. The result is that half of the healthy fatty acids are lost in the milling process, as well as the wheat germ and bran, which contain vitamins and fiber. By removing most of the naturally occurring nutrients and adding chemicals and a few isolated and synthetic vitamins and minerals, we've managed to take a healthy food that's been on families' tables for centuries—usually in the form of bread, pasta, or baked goods—and turn it into one of the most highly allergenic, difficult-to-digest substances available.

The healthier alternative is eating whole wheat bread and other whole grain products made from unprocessed whole grain flour that is preferably sprouted or sour leavened.

6. White sugar. Sugar may be as big a villain in raising blood pressure as salt, says Harry G. Preuss, M.D., of Georgetown University Medical School. In studies with laboratory test animals, Dr. Preuss found that salt and sugar together boost blood pressure more than either alone. Sugar appeared to disrupt the metabolism of insulin, a hormone that helps regulate blood pressure. Also, heavy consumption of sugar induces salt and water retention.[14]

Sugar comes in so many forms that it's hard to keep track of the names used for it these days. If the food label utilizes descriptions like corn syrup, high-fructose corn syrup, sucrose, corn sweeteners, sorghum syrup, or fruit juice concentrate, you're essentially eating sugar.

7. Soft drinks. Nothing more than liquefied sugar, a twenty-ounce Coke or Pepsi is the equivalent of eating fifteen teaspoons of sugar. Diet drinks loaded with artificial sweeteners are even worse.

8. Corn syrup. This is another version of refined sugar and just as bad for you, if not worse.

9. Pasteurized homogenized skimmed milk. As I said, whole, organic, nonhomogenized milk is better, and goat's milk is best.

10. Hydrolyzed soy protein. Hydrolyzed soy protein is found in imitation meat products such as imitation crab. I would look at hydrolyzed soy protein as I would regard processed meats heavy in sodium: stay away from them. You're always going to be better off eating organic meats.

11. Conventional table salt. Toss the regular salt shaker into the trash with a Joe Montana-style throw, and replace your table salt with Herbamare or one of the organic salts like Celtic Sea Salt or RealSalt.

12. Anything fried in unhealthy oils. Fried foods and high blood pressure go together like . . . cheeseburgers topped with bacon.

EAT: WHAT FOODS ARE EXTRAORDINARY, AVERAGE, OR TROUBLE?

I've prepared a comprehensive list of foods that are ranked in descending order based on their health-giving qualities. Foods at the top of the list are healthier than those at the bottom. The best foods to serve and eat are what I call "Extraordinary," which God created for us to eat and will give you the best chance to live a long and happy life. If you are battling high blood pressure, it's best to consume foods from the "Extraordinary" category more than 75 percent of the time.

Foods in the "Average" category should make up less than 25 percent of your daily diet. If your blood pressure numbers are too high, these foods should be consumed sparingly. Foods in the "Trouble" category should be consumed with extreme caution. If you're dealing with persistent hypertension, you should avoid these foods completely.

For a complete listing of Extraordinary, Average, and Trouble Foods, visit www.BiblicalHealthInstitute.com.

℞ THE GREAT PHYSICIAN'S RX FOR HIGH BLOOD PRESSURE: EAT TO LIVE

- *Eat only foods God created.*

- *Eat foods in a form that is healthy for the body.*

- *Consume foods high in omega-3 fatty acids such as wild-caught fish and organic eggs.*

- *Consume foods high in fiber.*

- *Increase consumption of raw fruits and vegetables.*

- *Increase consumption of leafy greens, grass-fed red meat, and high omega-3 eggs.*

- *Practice fasting one day per week.*

- *Drink eight or more glasses of pure water per day.*

- *Eliminate consumption of table salt and decrease overall consumption of sodium, replacing table salt with whole salt, spice combinations, or both.*

- *Avoid foods high in sugar.*

- *Avoid foods containing hydrogenated oils.*

Take Action

To learn how to incorporate the principles of eating to live into your daily lifestyle, please turn to page 75 for the Great Physician's Rx for High Blood Pressure Battle Plan.

KEY #2

Supplement Your Diet with Whole Food Nutritionals, Living Nutrients, and Superfoods

The crux of the DASH eating plan—Dietary Approaches to Stop Hypertension—is that you should stick to low-sodium foods high in potassium, calcium, and magnesium as a means of controlling your blood pressure. Scientists say a lack of these nutrients triggers high blood pressure in individuals. For example, researchers at the State University of New York found that the lower the level of magnesium in the body, the higher the blood pressure.[1]

As mentioned in Key #1, poultry, fish, bananas, cantaloupe, lima beans, milk, potatoes, and spinach are just a few of the high-potassium foods that should be part of your diet. Dairy products such as milk, yogurt, and cheese are good sources of calcium, and magnesium is found in whole grains, green leafy vegetables, black beans, and certain nuts.

Even if you're making a concerted effort to shop for and cook grass-fed beef and free-range chicken, as well as eat cultured dairy products and organic fruits and vegetables, you still won't be receiving the nutrients that you should, because today's foods have been depleted by nutrient-barren soils. That's why I believe you should cover your bases by taking nutritional supplements, which offer a concentrated source of nutrients that today's animal and plant foods don't always provide.

To carry the baseball metaphor a step further, three of the

bases that high blood pressure sufferers need to cover are potassium, calcium, and magnesium, the same trio of minerals recognized by the DASH diet in controlling blood pressure. But don't go running to your local health food store and sweep bottles of potassium, magnesium, or calcium supplements off the shelves. Instead, you can receive these useful nutrients by taking nutritional supplements from "whole food" sources that will supply your body with all the potassium, magnesium, and calcium firepower you'll need.

"Whole food" or "living" supplements contain various compounds such as organic acids, antioxidants, and key nutrients. They are produced with raw materials made from adding vitamins and minerals to a living probiotic culture. Whole food supplements are more costly to produce because the ingredients—fruits, vegetables, vitamins, minerals, and so on—are put through a fermentation process similar to the digestive process of the body.

That's why whole food multivitamins are several leagues higher than commercially produced multivitamins, which are synthetically made or isolated by using laboratory-manufactured nutrients that aren't identical, molecularly speaking, to natural nutrients. Synthetic and isolated versions of multivitamins and other minerals are much cheaper to produce, but they are nutritional folly because they skip the entire process of nature.

For recommendations on purchasing whole food multivitamins containing highly absorbable potassium, magnesium, and calcium, visit www.BiblicalHealthInstitute.com and click on the GPRx Resource Guide.

Green Foods

The next supplement I advise for those suffering from high blood pressure are green foods, which are also known as "superfoods."

I mentioned in Key #1 that vegetables—especially the green, leafy kind—are excellent sources of potassium and magnesium. Many people nod their heads in agreement, but a dislike of eating vegetables has followed them into adulthood. They *know* they should eat more vegetables, but they regard broccoli, green beans, and robust salads as colorful decorations for the main event—the meat and potatoes. If you feel this way, you're not alone: the United States Department of Agriculture estimates that more than 90 percent of the US population fail to eat the recommended three to five servings of vegetables and fruits each day.

You're not going to lower your blood pressure by picking at your vegetables and leafy salads. A way to ensure that you receive enough potassium, magnesium, and calcium is through the consumption of green superfood powders and caplets, which are an excellent way to get the vitamins, minerals, antioxidants, and enzymes found in green leafy vegetables. All you do is mix green superfood powder in water or juice, or you can choose to swallow a handful of caplets.

A quality green-food supplement is a certified organic blend of dried green vegetables, dried cereal grass juices from barley and wheatgrass, fermented vegetables, sea vegetables, microalgaes such as spirulina and chlorella, and sprouted grains and seeds—and very low in sodium. If you mix a couple of scoops of green-food powder into a glass of water or juice, you'll be drinking one of the most nutrient-dense foods on this green earth.

OMEGA-3 COD LIVER OIL

In Key #1, I discussed the importance of eating wild-caught fish because they are high in omega-3 fatty acids. Well, one of the best nutritional sources of omega-3 fatty acids is cod liver oil. This All-Star supplement is known for lowering blood pressure, controlling cholesterol, and making the arteries more flexible.

One study that looked at the incidence of high blood pressure and omega-3 fatty acids in large populations suggested that diets high in omega-3 fatty acids did lower blood pressure readings, according to Japanese researchers at the University of Hokkaido.[2] Furthermore, consuming omega-3 cod liver oil improves cardiovascular function by widening blood vessels and keeping blood platelets from clotting together inside the arterial walls.[3] When passages open and blood flows more freely, this places less pressure on the heart to work hard.

Those with high blood pressure often have high levels of fat in their blood, which means they also travel through life with low levels of HDL, the "good" cholesterol. Sipping spoonfuls or taking liquid capsules of omega-3 cod liver oil daily helps keep the high levels of fat in blood cells—known as triglycerides—in check and may inhibit the progression of cardiovascular disease.

The best type of fish oil to add to your daily nutritional regime is omega-3 cod liver oil extracted from cod taken from the freezing waters of the North Atlantic. The golden oils extracted from the filleted livers of cod may be an acquired taste, but after a decade of sipping spoonfuls of cod liver oil, I'm at the point where I can drink the stuff right out of the bottle.

If you can't stomach the thought of sipping omega-3 cod liver oil, you can now take this important nutrient in easy-to-swallow liquid capsules. (For recommended brands, visit www.Biblical HealthInstitute.com and click on the GPRx Resource Guide.)

ANTIOXIDANT SUPPLEMENTS

Antioxidants such as vitamins C and E, as well as extracts from fruits, vegetables, and spices, help blood vessels dilate and improve the stability of blood vessel walls, factors that help reduce high blood pressure numbers. Though I'm not a believer in taking vitamin C in massive amounts because of the possible side effects like diarrhea, the judicious intake of antioxidants like vitamin C and vitamin E can mitigate high blood pressure problems, according to a University of California at Irvine study several years ago. Nostratola D. Vaziri, M.D., the study's lead author, said that antioxidants can help reduce high blood pressure by protecting the body's supply of nitric oxide, which is a molecule that relaxes blood vessels.[4]

Another antioxidant, grape seed extract, found enthusiasts after a 2006 study by scientists at the University of California at Davis discovered that blood pressure levels fell for the group taking grape seed extract. Systolic blood pressure (the first number in a blood pressure reading) dropped by twelve points, on average, and diastolic blood pressure (the second number in a reading) dropped by an average of eight points.[5]

Pomegranate extract is emerging as another fighter of high blood pressure. Several compounds in pomegranate have been found by scientists to be powerful antioxidants that can disrupt the biochemicals contributing to high blood pressure.[6] According to *Life Extension* magazine, "Scientists believe that pomegranate, a potent source of antioxidants, may promote healthy blood pressure levels by enhancing the activity and preventing the degradation of an important vasodilating agent."[7] However, you're better off taking a pomegranate extract than eating pomegranates or drinking their juice because an extract contains virtually no calories or sugar.

Other supplements raising hopes are an isolated milk protein known as C_{12} peptide and coenzyme Q_{10}, which are being studied for their blood pressure lowering benefits. If you're battling high blood pressure, research these nutrients on the Internet. They may help you safely and effectively drag those high blood pressure numbers down to healthy levels.

Finally, there are two additional nutritionals I want to mention—a pair of adaptogenic herbs that could lower your blood pressure: the eastern Indian herb *Ashwaghandha* and the Russian herb *Rhodiola rosea*. When mixed into hot water, like tea, or taken as a dietary supplement, these adaptogenic herbs revitalize metabolic processes and moderate stress levels by working to bring the body back into balance.

℞ THE GREAT PHYSICIAN'S RX FOR HIGH BLOOD PRESSURE: SUPPLEMENT YOUR DIET

- *Take a whole food living multivitamin with each meal.*

- *Mix green superfood powder in water or juice twice per day, morning and evening, or you can choose to swallow a handful of caplets.*

- *Consume one to three teaspoons or three to nine capsules of omega-3 cod liver oil per day.*

- *Add an antioxidant supplement containing grape and pomegranate extracts to your nutritional regimen to lower blood pressure.*

Take Action

To learn how to incorporate the principles of supplementing your diet with whole food nutritionals, living nutrients, and superfoods into your daily lifestyle, please turn to page 75 for the Great Physician's Rx for High Blood Pressure Battle Plan.

KEY #3

Practice Advanced Hygiene

I will be the first to admit that dipping your face into a basin of facial solution, cleaning under your fingernails with a special soap, or washing your hands after going to the bathroom doesn't sound like it has much to do with high blood pressure. But there's an aspect to good hygiene that's relevant to this discussion, and it has to do with the link between inflammation and hypertension.

First, a little high school biology lesson.

Every day of your life, your body wards off gazillions of germs, which break down your immune system and make you more susceptible to health problems. Every *other* day of your life (or so it seems), little "ow-ees" happen: a badly stubbed toe, mosquito bite, slight sunburn, pulled muscle, or nick while shaving your legs (for you gals) or your face (for you guys). Whenever any of these scenarios happen, the body mounts an instantaneous defense, sending cells and natural chemicals to assault those nasty flu germs or repair the slight gash in your skin. Scientifically speaking, this response is known as *inflammation.*

Most people think inflammation is something that happens to your back after digging up weeds all Saturday morning. Actually, inflammation can occur when viruses invade the respiratory system or you wolf down a bad hot dog from a street vendor, for example. When events like these happen, the body launches a counterattack that lays waste to outside intruders or repairs any infected bodily organs.

When inflammation occurs, the liver produces a protein known as high-sensitivity C-reactive protein. This natural chemical is released into the bloodstream to help the body fight flu germs, for example, or repair itself after you pull a splinter out of your index finger. What medical researchers are learning, however, is that there is a strong link between high C-reactive protein levels and the future development of high blood pressure.

Researchers from Harvard Medical School and Harvard-affiliated Brigham and Women's Hospital conducted research that provided evidence for the first time that high blood pressure may be an inflammatory disease. If that's the case, inflammation contributes to a rise in blood pressure by promoting changes in the endothelium, which lines the walls of the blood vessels.[1]

This is noteworthy because Key #3 of *The Great Physician's Rx for High Blood Pressure*, "Practice Advanced Hygiene," can protect your body from becoming chronically inflamed, which will lower your C-reactive protein levels as well as lower your risk of developing high blood pressure.

What do I mean by the phrase "advanced hygiene"?

I'm glad you asked, because I'm a great believer in protecting myself from harmful germs, and I've been practicing an advanced hygiene protocol for more than a decade. I've witnessed the results in my own life: no lingering head colds, no nagging sinus infections, no acute respiratory illnesses to speak of for many years, and hopefully no high blood pressure in my future.

I follow a program first developed by Australian scientist

Kenneth Seaton, Ph.D., who discovered that ear, nose, throat, and skin problems could be linked to the fact that humans touch their noses, eyes, ears, and mouths with germ-carrying fingernails throughout the day.

In scientific terms, this is known as auto- or self-inoculation. So how do your fingernails get dirty? Through hand-to-hand contact with surfaces and other people. If you thought that most germs were spread by airborne exposure—someone sneezing at your table—you would be wrong. "Germs don't fly, they hitch-hike," Dr. Seaton declared, and he's right.

Dr. Seaton estimates that once you pick up hitchhiking germs, they hibernate and hide around the fingernails, no matter how short you keep them trimmed. You would be surprised to find out how much you constantly scratch your nose or rub your mouth and eyes, but if you're like most people, it's a frequent habit. When you come into contact with contagious germs, you can get sick, come down with the common cold, or find yourself battling the flu. This happens all the time. Chuck Gerba, a University of Arizona environmental-microbiology professor, says that 80 percent of infections, from cold and flu viruses to food-borne diseases, are spread through contact with hands and surfaces.

How do you get germs on your hands? By shaking hands with others or touching things they touched: handrails, door-knobs, shopping carts, paper money, coins, and food. I know this isn't pleasant dinner conversation, but practicing advanced hygiene has become an everyday habit for me.

Since I'm aware that 90 percent of germs take up residence around my fingernails, I use a creamy, semisoft soap rich in essential oils. Each morning and evening, I dip both of my hands into the tub of semisoft soap and dig my fingernails into the cream. Then I work the special cream around the tips of my fingers, cuticles, and fingernails for fifteen to thirty seconds. When I'm finished, I wash my hands under running water, lathering them for fifteen seconds before rinsing. After my hands are clean, I take another dab of semisoft soap and wash my face.

My next step involves a procedure that I call a "facial dip." I fill my washbasin or a clean large bowl with warm but not hot water. When enough water is in the basin, I add one to two tablespoons of regular table salt and two eyedroppers of a mineral-based facial solution into the cloudy water. I mix everything with my hands, and then I bend over and dip my face into the cleansing liquid, opening my eyes several times to allow the membranes to be cleansed. After coming up for air, I dunk my head a second time and blow bubbles through my nose. "Sink snorkeling," I call it.

My final two steps of advanced hygiene involve the application of very diluted drops of hydrogen peroxide and minerals into my ears for thirty to sixty seconds to cleanse the ear canal, followed by brushing my teeth with an essential-oil tooth solution to cleanse my teeth, gums, and mouth of unhealthy germs. (For more information on my favorite advanced hygiene products, visit www.BiblicalHealthInstitute.com and click on the GPRx Resource Guide.)

Brushing your teeth well and regularly practicing advanced hygiene involves discipline; you have to remind yourself to do it until it becomes an ingrained habit. I find it easier to follow these steps in the morning when I'm freshly awake than later in the evening when I'm tired and bleary-eyed—although I do my best to practice advanced hygiene every morning and every evening. Either way, I know it only takes three minutes or so to complete all of the advanced hygiene steps, and those might be the best three minutes of the day for your blood pressure.

A Primer on Washing Your Hands

1. Wet your hands with warm water. It doesn't have to be anywhere near scalding hot.

2. Apply plenty of soap into the palms of both hands. The best soap to use is a semisoft soap that you can dig your fingernails into.

3. Rub your hands vigorously together and scrub all the surfaces. Pay attention to the skin between the fingers, and work the soap into the fingernails.

4. Rub and scrub for fifteen to thirty seconds, or about the time it takes to slowly sing "Happy Birthday."

5. Rinse well and dry your hands on a paper towel or clean cloth towel. If you're in a public restroom, it's a good idea to turn off the running water with the towel in your hand. An even *better* idea is to use that same towel to open the door, since that door handle is the first place that nonwashers touch after they've gone to the bathroom.

6. Keep waterless sanitizers in your purse or wallet in case soap and water are not available in the public restroom. These towelettes, although not ideal, are better than nothing.

When to Wash Your Hands

- after you go to the bathroom
- before and after you insert or remove contact lenses
- before and after food preparation
- before you eat
- after you sneeze, cough, or blow your nose
- after cleaning up after your pet
- after handling money
- after changing a diaper
- after wiping a child's nose
- after handling garbage
- after cleaning your toilets
- after shaking hands
- after shopping at the supermarket
- after attending an event at a public theater
- before and after sexual intercourse

℞ THE GREAT PHYSICIAN'S RX FOR HIGH BLOOD PRESSURE: PRACTICE ADVANCED HYGIENE

- *Dig your fingers into a semisoft soap with essential oils, and wash your hands regularly, paying special attention to removing germs from underneath your fingernails.*

- *Cleanse your nasal passageways and the mucous membranes of your eyes daily by performing a facial dip.*

- *Cleanse the ear canals at least twice per week.*

- *Use an essential-oil-based tooth solution daily to remove germs from the teeth, gums, and mouth.*

Take Action

To learn how to incorporate the principles of practicing advanced hygiene into your daily lifestyle, please turn to page 75 for the Great Physician's Rx for High Blood Pressure Battle Plan.

KEY #4

Condition Your Body
with Exercise and Body Therapies

High blood pressure and exercise are like the chicken-or-the-egg conundrum: Do people develop high blood pressure because they don't exercise, or do folks not feel like exercising because they have hypertension?

While the causes of high blood pressure remain unknown and the condition doesn't exhibit any warning signs or symptoms, some can look back and say that they experienced headaches, dizziness, and times of fatigue before they learned about their diagnosis. In other words, they felt out of shape, winded after climbing two sets of stairs, and too tired to do chores around the house.

The most important thing you can do—besides changing your diet to the Great Physician's prescription eating plan—is to start faithfully exercising. By "faithfully exercising," I mean thirty minutes of physical activity five times a week. The idea is to get your heartbeat up for at least twenty minutes every time you exercise. You must do this because the heart is your ultimate muscle, and exercise preserves and protects the quality of the heart's blood vessels. Regular, consistent exercise almost always does a heart good. You'll live longer, lower blood pressure, and improve cardiovascular circulation. A solid body of evidence shows that men and women of all ages who are physically active have a decreased risk of developing hypertension. In a study of 902 people with hypertension, between forty-five and sixty-nine years old, positive long-term effects on blood pressure and cholesterol levels were achieved through increased exercise combined with a lower-fat diet.[1]

When it comes to high blood pressure and Key #4, "Condition Your Body with Exercise and Body Therapies," you don't want to wait for a blood pressure reading of 180/110 to get your attention. You want to get those feet—and arms—moving right away, or there might not be another blood pressure reading.

I have a background in physical fitness, having been a personal trainer at one time. If you were my client, having been informed by your doctor that you must begin an exercise program, I would start with *functional fitness.* This form of gentle exercise will raise your heartbeat, strengthen the body's core muscles, and exercise the cardiovascular system through the performance of real-life activities in real-life positions.

Functional fitness can be done with no equipment or by employing dumbbells, mini-trampolines, and stability balls. You can find functional fitness classes and equipment at gyms around the country, including LA Fitness, Bally Total Fitness, and local YMCAs. You'll be asked to perform squats with feet apart, with feet together, and with one back and the other forward. You'll be asked to do reaching lunges, push-ups against a wall, and "supermans" that involve lying on the floor and lifting up your right arm while lifting your left leg into a fully extended position. What you *won't* be asked to perform are high-impact exercises like those found in pulsating aerobics classes. (For more information on functional fitness, visit BiblicalHealthInstitute.com and click on the GPRx Resource Guide.)

Breathe Right

You might want to sit up and take a deep breath when you hear about this: Dr. David Anderson, who heads research on hypertension at the NIH National Institute on Aging, suggests that breathing slowly—taking fewer than ten breaths per minute—can help some people nudge down bad blood pressure, but more study needs to be done before definitive statements can be made.[2]

Researchers agree, however, that deep-breathing exercises enrich the cardiovascular system. Most of the time, we don't completely fill the diaphragm with air because we're not aware that our lungs hang all the way to the bottom of the rib cage. I recommend sitting in a chair and concentrating on filling the lungs completely. Count to five as you breathe in, then hold your breath for several seconds before exhaling through your mouth for several more seconds. Visualize your diaphragm moving up and down as your lungs expand. Deep-breathing techniques are a peaceful, powerful tool to calm your nervous system, slow down your heartbeat, and restore your energy. And if your blood pressure levels sink, so much the better.

I would also incorporate these forms of exercise and physical therapies in your fight to bring your blood pressure down:

1. *Walk up a storm.* Walking is especially good for those who've been lax in working out over the years. This low-impact route to

fitness places a gentle strain on the hips and the rest of the body, and when done briskly, makes the heart work harder and expend more energy.

Best of all, you can walk when it fits your schedule—before work, on your lunch hour, before dinner, or after dinner. You set the pace; you decide how much you put into this exercise. Walking is a great social exercise that allows you to carry on a civilized conversation with a friend or loved one.

> ### Time to Quit
>
> Still smoking? Although smoking injures blood vessel walls and speeds up the process of hardening the arteries, it is not an official cause of high blood pressure. Still, my thinking is that if there's smoke, there's fire . . .

2. *Go to bed earlier.* Sleep is a body therapy in short supply these days. A nationwide "sleep deficit" means that we're packing in as much as we can from the moment we wake up until we crawl into bed sixteen, seventeen, or eighteen exhausting hours later. American adults are down to a little less than seven hours of sleep each night, a good two hours less than our great-great-grandparents slept a hundred years ago.

How many hours of sleep are you getting nightly? The magic number is eight hours, say the sleep experts. That's because when people are allowed to sleep as much as they would like in a controlled setting, like in a sleep laboratory, they naturally sleep eight hours in a twenty-four-hour time period.

This is a good time to talk about sleep apnea and how it relates to high blood pressure. Sleep apnea is a serious, potentially life-threatening condition characterized by brief interruptions in breathing during sleep. Those with sleep apnea are often unaware that they wheeze and snore throughout the night, only to have their breathing suddenly stop for a long moment. You can only imagine the havoc that low oxygen levels wreak on the heart and lungs—or the worry it causes your spouse.

High blood pressure is clearly linked to sleep apnea, says the Mayo Clinic, but precisely why the two are linked is still unknown. If your snoring knocks family photos off the wall, or your spouse comments about momentary pauses in your breathing, seek medical attention right away. You may require a special pressure-generating machine to help control your sleep apnea and lower your blood pressure levels.

3. *Rest on the seventh day.* In addition to proper sleep, the body needs a time of rest every seven days to recharge its batteries. This is accomplished by taking a break from the rat race on Saturday or Sunday. God created the earth and the heavens in six days and rested on the seventh, giving us an example and a reminder that we need to take a break from our labors. Otherwise, we're prime candidates for burnout.

4. *Let the sun shine in.* You may not see much correlation between sunning yourself and high blood pressure, but let me explain: When your face or your arms and legs are exposed to sunlight, your skin synthesizes vitamin D from the ultraviolet

rays of sunlight. The body needs vitamin D, which is not actually a vitamin but a critical hormone that helps regulate the health of more than thirty different tissues and organs, including the heart's cardiovascular system. I recommend intentionally exposing yourself to at least fifteen minutes of sunlight a day to increase vitamin D levels in the body.

5. *Treat yourself to hydrotherapy.* Hydrotherapy comes in the form of baths, showers, washing, and wraps—using hot *and* cold water. For instance, I wake up with a hot shower in the mornings, but then I turn off the hot water and stand under the brisk, cold water for about a minute, which totally invigorates me. Cold water stimulates the body and boosts oxygen use in the cells, while hot water dilates blood vessels, which in effect lowers blood pressure.

What about saunas? After all, many public saunas carry a health warning that those with high blood pressure or a heart condition should exercise caution. Ask your physician what he or she thinks, but I would think that since the intense heat in a sauna causes the capillaries in the skin to dilate, which lowers blood pressure, this would be a good thing. Just be sure to drink plenty of pure water during the sauna to replace fluids lost during perspiration.

I'm a fan of far-infrared saunas, which provide a comfortable and simple way to improve health while gently raising the heart rate, and regular users have reported an improvement in skin tone and a lessening of aches and pains. I have owned and used a far-infrared sauna for more than eight years and highly recommend it. (For more information on far-infrared sauna technology, visit www.BiblicalHealthInstitute.com.)

6. *Finally, pamper yourself with aromatherapy and music therapy.* In aromatherapy, essential oils from plants, flowers, and spices are introduced to your skin and pores either by rubbing them in or inhaling their aromas. The use of these essential oils will not miraculously repair blocked coronary arteries, but they will give you an emotional lift. Try rubbing a few drops of myrtle, coriander, hyssop, galbanum, or frankincense onto the palms, then cup your hands over your mouth and nose and inhale. A deep breath will invigorate the spirit.

Listening to soft and soothing music promotes relaxation and healing. I know what I like when it comes to music therapy: contemporary praise and worship music. No matter what works for you, you'll find that listening to uplifting mood music can heal the body, soul, and spirit.

℞ THE GREAT PHYSICIAN'S RX FOR HIGH BLOOD PRESSURE: CONDITION YOUR BODY WITH EXERCISE AND BODY THERAPIES

- *Make a commitment and an appointment to exercise five times a week for at least thirty minutes.*

- *Incorporate five to fifteen minutes of functional fitness into your daily schedule.*

- *Take a brisk walk and see how much better you feel at the end of the day.*

- *Make a conscious effort to practice deep-breathing exercises once a day. Inflate your lungs to full and hold for several seconds before slowly exhaling.*

- *Go to sleep earlier, paying close attention to how much sleep you get before midnight. Do your best to get eight hours of sleep nightly. Sleep is the most important non-nutrient you can incorporate into your health regimen.*

- *End your shower by changing the water temperature to cool (or cold) and standing underneath the spray for one minute.*

- *Once a week, take a day of rest. Dedicate the day to the Lord and do something fun and relaxing that you haven't done in a while. Make your rest day work-free, errand-free, and shop-free. Trust God that He'll do more with His six days than you can do with seven.*

- *For fiteen minutes each day, sit outside in a chair and face the sun. Aviod exposure between the hours of 10 a.m. and 2 p.m., when the sin's rays are at their peak.*

- *Incorporate essential oils into your daily life.*

- *Play worship music in your home, in your car, or on your iPod. Focus on God's plan for your life.*

Take Action

To learn how to incorporate the principles of conditioning your body with exercise and body therapies into your daily lifestyle, please turn to page 75 for the Great Physician's Rx for High Blood Pressure Battle Plan.

KEY #5

Reduce Toxins in Your Environment

Although modern medicine has yet to establish a clear link between high blood pressure and environmental factors like pollution or toxins, common sense tells me that breathing polluted air, bathing in chlorinated water, consuming high-mercury fish, and eating pesticide-laden fruits and vegetables will not benefit your cardiovascular system nor the arterial vessels transporting blood from your heart to the outer extremities of your body.

You're probably aware that we live in a toxic world where the prudent should protect themselves from chemicals, pollutants, and industrial compounds present in the food we eat, the air we breathe, the water we drink, the skin and body care products we use, and the everyday household products we come into physical contact with. The problem is that it's impossible *not* to come into close contact with health-threatening toxins in our environment.

Thankfully God, in His infinite wisdom, designed the body so that the liver, kidneys, and skin can eliminate internal toxins through the bowels, urine, and sweat. If toxins overburden any of these organs, however, the body goes off-kilter. One sign of things not being right is high blood pressure.

The chemical residues inside our bodies are referred to by scientists as a person's *body burden*. How much body burden do

Some toxins are water soluble, meaning they are rapidly passed out of the body and present no harm. Unfortunately, many more toxins are fat soluble, meaning that it can take months or years before they are completely eliminated from your system. Some of the more well-known fat-soluble toxins are dioxins, phthalates, and chlorine, and when they are not eliminated from the body, they become stored in your fatty tissues and clog your arteries—a made-to-order recipe for hypertension.

The best way to flush fat-soluble toxins out of your blood-stream is to increase your intake of pure drinking water, which helps eliminate toxins through the kidneys. Drinking more water will speed up your metabolism and allow your body to assimilate nutrients from the foods you eat and the nutritional supplements you take. Since water is the primary resource for carrying nutrients throughout the body and removing waste from our cells, a lack of adequate hydration results in metabolic wastes assaulting your body—a form of self-poisoning.

That's why the importance of drinking enough water cannot be overstated: water is a life force involved in nearly every bodily process, from digestion to blood circulation. Your heart pumps blood much more efficiently when you're well hydrated, which will do wonders for your high blood pressure. Nothing beats plain old water—a liquid created by God to be totally compatible with your body. My recommendation is that you should drink a half ounce of water per pound of body weight, meaning if you weigh 150 pounds, you should be drinking seventy-five ounces of water daily.

I don't recommend drinking water straight from the tap,

you have? What's the tipping point when your body can't pr[
erly handle everything that comes its way?

Nobody's sure, which is a problem.

That's why it's important to take steps to reduce your b[
burden as well the body burdens of family members around y[
The first place to start is with the *indoor* air you're breathing. [
you heard me right. The American Lung Association estimates t[
we spend 90 percent of our time indoors, breathing recirculat[
air-conditioned air in the summer and heated air in the winte[
air swirling with toxic particles. Today's well-insulated homes [
energy-efficient doors and windows trap "used" air filled with [
bon dioxide, nitrogen dioxide, and pet dander. These polluta[
trigger and accelerate narrowing of carotid arteries, and that c[
be good for those with high blood pressure.

I recommend opening your doors and windows periodically[
freshen the air you breathe, even if the temperatures are blazing [
or downright freezing. Just a few minutes of fresh air will do w[
ders. I also recommend that you purchase a quality air filter, wh[
will remove and neutralize tiny airborne particles of dust, so[
pollen, mold, and dander. I have set up four high-quality air pu[
fiers in our home that scrub harmful impurities out of the air.

Chemicals and toxins dangerous to heart health are also pr[
ent in our food supply. If your blood and urine were tested, l[
technicians would uncover dozens of toxins in your bloodstrea[
including PCBs (polychlorinated biphenyls), dioxins, furans, tra[
metals, phthalates, VOCs (volatile organic compounds), ar[
chlorine.

however. Nearly all municipal water is routinely treated with chlorine or chloramine, potent bacteria-killing chemicals. I've installed a whole-house filtration system that removes the chlorine and other impurities out of the water *before* it enters our household pipes. My wife, Nicki, and I can confidently turn on the tap and enjoy the health benefits of chemical-, germ-, and chlorine-free water for drinking, cooking, and bathing. Since our water doesn't have a chemical aftertaste, we're more apt to drink it.

Besides drinking plenty of water, you must increase the fiber in your diet to eliminate toxins through the bowels, exercise and sweat to eliminate toxins through the lymphatic system, and practice deep breathing to eliminate toxins through the lungs. You can also reduce the number of toxins in your body by consuming organic or grass-fed meat and dairy products.

Remember: most commercially produced beef and chicken act as chemical magnets for toxins in the environment, so they will not be as healthy as eating organic grass-fed meats. In addition, consuming organic produce purchased at health food stores, roadside stands, and farmer's markets (only if produce is grown locally and unsprayed) will expose you to less pesticide residues, as compared to conventionally grown fruits and vegetables.

Canned tuna is another food to eat minimally, although many popular diets include tuna and salad as a lunchtime or dinner staple. Metallic particles of mercury, lead, and aluminum continue to be found in the fatty tissues of tuna, swordfish, and king mackerel. Shrimp and lobster, which are shellfish that scavenge the ocean floor, are unclean meats that should be eliminated from your diet. I recommend you limit the consumption of conventional canned tuna to two cans per week and avoid shellfish completely. (For recommendations on low-mercury, high omega-3 tuna, please visit www.BiblicalHealthInstitute.com and click on the GPRx Resource Guide.)

TOXINS ELSEWHERE IN YOUR ENVIRONMENT

There are other toxins that are not directly related to high blood pressure but are important enough to mention:

- **Plastics.** Although I drink mineral waters from plastic containers when I'm not at home, I think it's safer to drink water from a glass because of the presence of dioxins and phthalates added in the manufacturing process of plastic.

- **Household cleaners.** Many of today's commercial house cleaners contain potentially harmful chemicals and solvents that expose people to VOCs—volatile organic compounds—which can cause eye, nose, and throat irritation.

  Nicki and I have found that natural ingredients like vinegar, lemon juice, and baking soda are excellent substances that make our home spick-and-span. Natural cleaning products that aren't harsh, abrasive, or potentially dangerous to your family are available in grocery and natural food stores.

- **Skin care and body care products.** Toxic chemicals such as chemical solvents and phthalates are found in lipstick, lip gloss, lip conditioner, hair coloring, hair spray, shampoo, and soap. Ladies, when you rub a tube of lipstick across your lips, your skin readily absorbs these toxins, and that's unhealthy. As with household cleaners, you can find natural cosmetics in natural food stores and progressive markets, although they are becoming more widely available in drugstores and beauty stores.

- **Toothpaste.** A tube of toothpaste contains a warning that in case of accidental swallowing, you should contact the local Poison Control Center. What's that all about? Most commercially available toothpastes contain artificial sweeteners, potassium nitrate, and a whole bunch of long, unpronounceable words. Again, search out a healthy, natural alternative.

Finally, let me pull the guys aside for a moment and talk about high blood pressure and . . . your sex life. If you've been having trouble . . . you know . . . performing, be aware that hypertension is one of the most closely linked conditions to erection problems. A study in the *Journal of American Geriatrics Society* found that 49 percent of men aged forty to seventy-nine with high blood pressure had erectile dysfunction.[1]

For men with high blood pressure, the arterial vessels that carry blood throughout the body can become damaged. This damage may include the vessels that carry blood to and from the penis, meaning it doesn't get enough blood to achieve or maintain an erection.

So if you were looking for something else to inspire you other than simply living longer, then let this be it.

℞ THE GREAT PHYSICIAN'S RX FOR HIGH BLOOD PRESSURE: REDUCE TOXINS IN YOUR ENVIRONMENT

- *Pay attention to the amount of air pollution inside and outside your home—especially if you are fighting cardiovascular disease.*

- *Drink a half ounce of water for every pound of body weight every day.*

- *Use glass containers instead of plastic containers whenever possible.*

- *Improve indoor air quality by opening windows, purchasing house plants, and buying an air filtration system.*

- *Use natural cleaning products for your home.*

- *Use natural products for skin care, body care, hair care, cosmetics, and toothpaste.*

Take Action

To learn how to incorporate the principles of reducing toxins in your environment, please turn to page 75 for the Great Physician's Rx for High Blood Pressure Battle Plan.

Key #6

Avoid Deadly Emotions

Do you have too much to do at home and at work?

Are the kids causing problems?

Not enough money and too many bills?

Feeling stressed out?

Got high blood pressure?

You would think that stress and high blood pressure go together like peanut butter and jelly. But the National Heart, Lung, and Blood Institute (NHLBI) says that, while stress has been long thought to contribute to high blood pressure, the long-term effects of stress are unclear. The Cleveland Clinic declared that while blood pressure increases when a person is under emotional stress and tension, there isn't enough evidence to conclude that psychological interventions aimed at stress reduction can decrease blood pressure in patients with hypertension.

Why do many in conventional medicine feel this way? Some doctors say that because a certain amount of stress is part of daily life, one learns to live with tension and nervous strain. But Don Colbert, M.D., and author of the fine book *Deadly Emotions,* says that it's becoming more and more apparent in his research that emotions such as stress, anger, acrimony, apprehension, agitation, anxiety, and alarm are powerful forces within the human mind that clearly affect the body and the soul. When someone's life is an emotional roller coaster, his or her physical and psychological vitality is sapped, which often leaves the body and mind depleted of energy and strength.

Dr. Colbert explains that:

- the mind and the body are linked, which means how you feel emotionally can determine how you feel physically;

- certain emotions release hormones into the body that can trigger the development of a host of diseases; and

- emotions such as anxiety and fear have been linked to heart palpitations, irritable bowel syndrome, tension headaches, and other diseases.[1]

Are you harboring resentment in your heart, nursing a grudge into overtime, or plotting revenge against those who hurt you? If you're still bottling up emotions such as anger, bitterness, and resentment, these deadly emotions will produce toxins similar to those you would get from bingeing on nachos and pizza.

Deadly emotions alter the chemistry of your body, and unchecked emotions can be a pervasive force in determining your daily behavior. Eating while under stress causes the liver's bile tubes to narrow, which blocks bile from reaching the small intestine, where food is waiting to be digested. This is not healthy for the body. An old proverb states it well: "What you are eating is not nearly as important as what's eating you."

This is the time to put your past in the rearview mirror and move forward. There may be someone you need to forgive. I learned this lesson once when I shared a meal with Bruce Wilkinson, the founder of Walk Thru the Bible ministries and author of the mega-bestseller *The Prayer of Jabez*. Over breakfast, he urged me to forgive those who had hurt me in the past by writing their names on a piece of paper and then stating, "I forgive you for . . ."

I balked at first, telling Dr. Wilkinson that I wasn't the type to hold grudges. But he persisted, asking me again, "Jordan, is there anyone in your life that you need to forgive?"

Actually, there were a couple of doctors who told me that my incurable illnesses were my fault. Several relatives and friends said they would be there for me when I first got sick, but I never heard from them again. Bruce Wilkinson was right: there were more people than I would have thought. After I dealt with each person, I bowed my head and asked God to help me forgive these people just as He forgives me for my sins. I prayed with a contrite heart, seeking His mercy and forgiveness.

As for you, please remember that no matter how badly you've been hurt in the past, it's still possible to forgive. "For if you forgive men their trespasses, your heavenly Father will also forgive you," Jesus said in Matthew 6. "But if you do not forgive men their trespasses, neither will your Father forgive your trespasses" (vv. 14–15 NKJV).

If you're angry, hurt, or bothered by those who've been mean to you, forgive them and then let it go. If you do, the next time you think of these people, instead of letting your blood boil, you may even see your blood pressure levels take a dive.

R℞ THE GREAT PHYSICIAN'S RX FOR HIGH BLOOD PRESSURE: AVOID DEADLY EMOTIONS

- *Recognize that deadly emotions can impact high blood pressure.*

- *Trust God when you face circumstances that cause you to worry or become anxious.*

- *Practice forgiveness every day, and forgive those who hurt you.*

Take Action

To learn how to incorporate the principles of avoiding deadly emotions into your daily lifestyle, please turn to page 75 for the Great Physician's Rx for High Blood Pressure Battle Plan.

THE GREAT PHYSICIAN'S RX
FOR HIGH BLOOD PRESSURE
BATTLE PLAN

DAY 1

Upon Waking

Prayer: thank God because this is the day the Lord has made. Rejoice and be glad in it. Thank Him for the breath in your lungs and the life in your body. Ask the Lord to heal your body and use your experience to benefit the lives of others. Read Matthew 6:9–13 aloud.

Purpose: ask the Lord to give you an opportunity to add significance to someone's life today. Watch for that opportunity. Ask God to use you this day for His intended purpose.

Advanced hygiene: for hands and nails, press fingers into semisoft soap four or five times, and lather hands with soap for fifteen seconds, rubbing soap over cuticles and rinsing under water as warm as you can stand. Take another swab of semisoft soap into your hands and wash your face. Next, fill a basin or sink with water as warm as you can stand, and add one to three tablespoons of table salt and one to three eyedroppers of iodine-based mineral solution. Dunk your face into the water and open your eyes, blinking repeatedly underwater. Keep your eyes open underwater for three seconds. After cleaning your eyes, put your face back in the water, and close your mouth while blowing bubbles out of your nose. Come up from the water, and immerse your face in the water once again, gently taking water into your nostrils and expelling bubbles. Come up from the water, and blow your nose into facial tissue.

To cleanse the ears, use hydrogen peroxide and mineral-based ear drops, putting two or three drops into each ear and letting stand for sixty seconds. Tilt your head to expel the drops.

For the teeth, apply two or three drops of essential-oil-based tooth drops to the toothbrush. This can be used to brush your teeth or added to existing toothpaste. After brushing your teeth, brush your tongue for fifteen seconds. (For recommended advanced hygiene products, visit www.BiblicalHealthInstitute.com and click on the Resource Guide.)

Reduce toxins: open your windows for one hour today. Use natural soap and natural skin- and body-care products (shower gel, body creams, etc.). Use natural facial-care products. Use natural toothpaste. Use natural hair-care products such as shampoo, conditioner, gel, mousse, and hairspray. (For recommended products, visit www.BiblicalHealth Institute.com and click on the Resource Guide.)

Supplements: take one serving of a fiber/green-superfood powder mixed into or five caplets of a super-green formula swallowed with twelve to sixteen ounces of water or raw vegetable juice. (For recommended products, visit www.BiblicalHealthInstitute.com and click on the Resource Guide.)

Body therapy: get twenty minutes of direct sunlight sometime during the day, but be careful between the hours of ten o'clock in the morning and two o'clock in the afternoon.

Exercise: perform functional fitness exercises for five to fifteen minutes or spend five to fifteen minutes on a mini-trampoline. Finish with five to ten minutes of deep-breathing exercises. (One to three rounds of the exercises can be found at www.BiblicalHealthInstitute.com.)

Emotional health: whenever you face a circumstance, such as your health, that causes you to worry, repeat the following: "Lord, I trust you. I cast my cares upon you, and I believe that you're going to take care of [insert your current situation] and make my health and my body strong." Confess that throughout the day whenever you think about your health condition.

Breakfast

Make a smoothie in a blender with the following ingredients:

1 cup organic plain yogurt (sheep's milk is best)

1 tablespoon organic flaxseed oil

1–2 tablespoons raw organic honey

1 cup of organic fruit (berries, banana, peaches, pineapple, etc.)

2 tablespoons goat's milk protein powder (for recommended brands, visit www.BiblicalHealthInstitute.com and click on the Resource Guide)

dash of vanilla extract (optional)

Supplements: take two whole food multivitamin caplets and one capsule of a whole food probiotic formula with soil-based organisms. (For recommended brands, visit www.BiblicalHealthInstitute.com and click on the Resource Guide.)

Lunch

Before eating, drink eight ounces of water.

During lunch, drink eight ounces of water, or hot or iced green tea with honey.

large green salad with mixed greens, avocado, carrots, cucumbers, celery, tomatoes, red cabbage, red peppers, red onions, and sprouts with three hard-boiled omega-3 eggs

salad dressing: mix extra-virgin olive oil, apple cider vinegar or lemon juice, minced fresh garlic, naturally brewed soy sauce, Celtic sea salt, herbs, and spices together; or, mix one tablespoon of extra-virgin olive oil with one tablespoon of a healthy store-bought dressing

one apple with skin

Supplements: take two whole food multivitamin caplets and one capsule of a whole food probiotic formula with soil-based organisms.

Dinner

Before eating, drink eight ounces of water.

During dinner, drink hot or iced green tea with honey. (For recommended brands, visit www.BiblicalHealthInstitute.com and click on the Resource Guide.)

baked, poached, or grilled wild-caught salmon

steamed broccoli

large green salad with mixed greens, avocado, carrots, tomato, red cabbage, red onions, red peppers, and sprouts.

salad dressing: mix extra-virgin olive oil, apple cider vinegar or lemon juice, minced fresh garlic, naturally brewed soy sauce, Celtic sea salt, herbs, and spices together; or, mix one tablespoon of extra-virgin olive oil with one tablespoon of a healthy store-bought dressing

Supplements: take two whole food multivitamin caplets and one capsule of a whole food probiotic with soil-based organisms and one to three teaspoons or three to nine capsules of a high omega-3 cod liver oil complex. (For recommended brands, visit www.BiblicalHealth Institute.com and click on the Resource Guide.)

Snacks

Drink eight to twelve ounces of water, or hot or iced green tea with honey. (For recommended brands, visit www.BiblicalHealthInstitute.com and click on the Resource Guide.)

apple slices with raw almond butter

one berry antioxidant whole food nutrition bar with beta-glucans from soluble oat fiber (for recommended brands, visit www.Biblical HealthInstitute.com and click on the Resource Guide)

Before Bed

Exercise: go for a walk outdoors or participate in a favorite sport or recreational activity.

Supplements: take one serving of a fiber/green-superfood powder mixed into, or five caplets of a super-green formula swallowed with, twelve to sixteen ounces of water or raw vegetable juice.

Body therapy: take a warm bath for fifteen minutes with eight drops of biblical essential oils added.

Advanced hygiene: repeat the advanced hygiene instructions from the morning.

Emotional health: ask the Lord to bring to your mind someone you need to forgive. Take a sheet of paper and write the person's name at the top. Try to remember each specific action that person did against you that brought you pain. Write down the following: "I forgive [insert person's name] for [insert the action he or she did against you]." After you fill the paper, tear it up or burn it, and ask God to give you the strength to truly forgive that person.

Purpose: ask yourself these questions: "Did I live a life of purpose today?" "What did I do to add value to someone else's life today?" Commit to living a day of purpose tomorrow.

Prayer: thank God for this day, asking Him to give you a restoring night's rest and a fresh start tomorrow. Thank Him for His steadfast love that never ceases and His mercies that are new every morning. Read Romans 8:35, 37–39 aloud.

Sleep: go to bed by half past ten.

Day 2

Upon Waking

Prayer: thank God because this is the day that the Lord has made. Rejoice and be glad in it. Thank Him for the breath in your lungs and the life in your body. Ask the Lord to heal your body and use your experience to benefit the lives of others. Read Psalm 91 aloud.

Purpose: ask the Lord to give you an opportunity to add significance to someone's life today. Watch for that opportunity. Ask God to use you this day for His intended purpose.

Advanced hygiene: follow the advanced hygiene recommendations from the morning of Day 1.

Reduce toxins: follow the recommendations to reduce toxins from the morning of Day 1.

Supplements: take one serving of a fiber/green-superfood powder mixed into, or five caplets of a super-green formula swallowed with, twelve to sixteen ounces of water or raw vegetable juice.

Body therapy: take a hot-and-cold shower. After a normal shower, alternate sixty seconds of water as hot as you can stand it, followed by sixty seconds of water as cold as you can stand it. Repeat cycle four times for a total of eight minutes, finishing with cold water.

Exercise: perform functional fitness exercises for five to fifteen minutes or spend five to fifteen minutes on a mini trampoline. Finish with five to ten minutes of deep-breathing exercises. (One to three rounds of the exercises can be found at www.BiblicalHealthInstitute.com.)

Emotional health: follow the emotional health recommendations from the morning of Day 1.

Breakfast

two or three eggs any style, cooked in one tablespoon of extra-virgin coconut oil (for recommended brands, visit www.BiblicalHealth Institute.com and click on the Resource Guide)

stir-fried onions, garlic, mushrooms, and peppers

one slice of sprouted or yeast-free whole grain bread with almond butter and honey

Supplements: take two whole food multivitamin caplets and one capsule of a whole food probiotic formula with soil-based organisms.

Lunch

Before eating, drink eight ounces of water.

During lunch, drink eight ounces of water, or hot or iced green tea with honey.

large green salad with mixed greens, avocado, carrots, tomato, red cabbage, red onions, red peppers, and sprouts, adding two ounces of low-mercury, high omega-3 tuna (for recommended brands, visit www.BiblicalHealthInstitute.com and click on the Resource Guide)

salad dressing: mix extra-virgin olive oil, apple cider vinegar or lemon juice, minced fresh garlic, naturally brewed soy sauce, Celtic sea salt, herbs, and spices together; or, mix one tablespoon of extra-virgin olive oil with one tablespoon of a healthy store-bought dressing

organic grapes

Supplements: take two whole food multivitamin caplets and one capsule of a whole food probiotic formula with soil-based organisms.

Dinner

Before eating, drink eight ounces of water.

During dinner, drink hot or iced green tea with honey.

roasted organic chicken

cooked vegetables (carrots, onions, garlic, peas, etc.)

large green salad with mixed greens, avocado, carrots, tomato, red cabbage, red onions, red peppers, and sprouts

salad dressing: mix extra-virgin olive oil, apple cider vinegar or lemon juice, minced fresh garlic, naturally brewed soy sauce, Celtic sea salt, herbs, and spices together; or, mix one tablespoon of extra-virgin olive oil with one tablespoon of a healthy store-bought dressing

Supplements: take two whole food multivitamin caplets and one capsule of a whole food probiotic formula with soil-based organisms and one to three teaspoons or three to nine capsules of a high omega-3 cod liver oil complex.

Snacks

Drink eight to twelve ounces of water, or hot or iced green tea with honey.

Mix one serving of a whole food meal supplement with beta-glucans from soluble oat fiber mixed in twelve to sixteen ounces of water. (For recommended brands, visit www.BiblicalHealthInstitute.com and click on the Resource Guide.)

one whole food nutrition bar with beta-glucans from soluble oat fiber

Before Bed

Exercise: go for a walk outdoors or participate in a favorite sport or recreational activity.

Supplements: take one serving of a fiber/green-superfood powder mixed into, or five caplets of a super-green formula swallowed with, twelve to sixteen ounces of water or raw vegetable juice.

Advanced hygiene: repeat the advanced hygiene instructions from the morning of Day 1.

Emotional health: repeat the emotional health recommendations from Day 1.

Purpose: ask yourself these questions: "Did I live a life of purpose today?" "What did I do to add value to someone else's life today?" Commit to living a day of purpose tomorrow.

Prayer: thank God for this day, asking Him to give you a restoring night's rest and a fresh start tomorrow. Thank Him for His steadfast love that never ceases and His mercies that are new every morning. Read 1 Corinthians 13:4–8 aloud.

Body therapy: spend ten minutes listening to soothing music before you retire.

Sleep: go to bed by half past ten.

DAY 3

Upon Waking

Prayer: thank God because this is the day the Lord has made. Rejoice and be glad in it. Thank Him for the breath in your lungs and the life in your body. Ask the Lord to heal your body and use your experience to benefit the lives of others. Read Ephesians 6:13–18 aloud.

Purpose: ask the Lord to give you an opportunity to add significance to someone's life today. Watch for that opportunity. Ask God to use you this day for His intended purpose.

Advanced hygiene: follow the advanced hygiene recommendations from the morning of Day 1.

Reduce toxins: follow the recommendations to reduce toxins from the morning of Day 1.

Supplements: take one serving of a fiber/green-superfood powder mixed into or five caplets of a super-green formula swallowed with twelve to sixteen ounces of water or raw vegetable juice.

Body therapy: get twenty minutes of direct sunlight sometime during the day, but be careful between the hours of ten o'clock in the morning and two o'clock in the afternoon.

Exercise: perform functional fitness exercises for five to fifteen minutes or spend five to fifteen minutes on a mini-trampoline. Finish with five to ten minutes of deep-breathing exercises. (One to three rounds of the exercises can be found at www.BiblicalHealthInstitute.com.)

Emotional Health: Follow the emotional health recommendations from Day 1.

Breakfast

Drink one cup of hot or iced green tea with honey.

four to eight ounces of organic whole milk yogurt or cottage cheese with fruit (pineapple, peaches, or berries), honey, and a dash of vanilla extract

handful of raw almonds

Supplements: take two whole food multivitamin caplets and one capsule of a whole food probiotic formula with soil-based organisms.

Lunch

Before eating, drink eight ounces of water.

During lunch, drink eight ounces of water, or hot or iced green tea with honey.

large green salad with mixed greens, avocado, carrots, tomato, red cabbage, red onions, red peppers, and sprouts with three hard-boiled omega-3 eggs

salad dressing: mix extra-virgin olive oil, apple cider vinegar or lemon juice, minced fresh garlic, naturally brewed soy sauce, Celtic sea salt, herbs, and spices together; or, mix one tablespoon of extra-virgin olive oil with one tablespoon of a healthy store-bought dressing

one piece of fruit in season

Supplements: take two whole food multivitamin caplets and one capsule of a whole food probiotic formula with soil-based organisms.

Dinner

Before eating, drink eight ounces of water.

During dinner, drink hot or iced green tea with honey.

red meat steak (beef, buffalo, or venison)

steamed broccoli

baked sweet potato with butter

large green salad with mixed greens, avocado, carrots, tomato, red cabbage, red onions, red peppers, and sprouts

salad dressing: mix extra-virgin olive oil, apple cider vinegar or lemon juice, minced fresh garlic, naturally brewed soy sauce, Celtic sea salt, herbs, and spices together; or, mix one tablespoon of extra-virgin olive oil with one tablespoon of a healthy store-bought dressing

Supplements: take two whole food multivitamin caplets and one capsule of a whole food probiotic formula with soil-based organisms and one to three teaspoons or three to nine capsules of a high omega-3 cod liver oil complex.

Snacks

Drink eight to twelve ounces of water, or hot or iced green tea with honey.

healthy chocolate (cacao) snack (for recommended brands, visit www.BiblicalHealthInstitute.com and click on Resource Guide)

one whole food nutrition bar with beta-glucans from soluble oat fiber

Before Bed

Exercise: go for a walk outdoors or participate in a favorite sport or recreational activity.

Supplements: take one serving of a fiber/green-superfood powder mixed into, or five caplets of a super-green formula swallowed with, twelve to sixteen ounces of water or raw vegetable juice.

Body therapy: take a warm bath for fifteen minutes with eight drops of biblical essential oils added.

Advanced hygiene: follow the advanced hygiene instructions from the morning of Day 1.

Emotional health: follow the forgiveness recommendations from the evening of Day 1.

Purpose: ask yourself these questions: "Did I live a life of purpose today?" "What did I do to add value to someone else's life today?" Commit to living a day of purpose tomorrow.

Prayer: thank God for this day, asking Him to give you a restoring night's rest and a fresh start tomorrow. Thank Him for His steadfast love that never ceases and His mercies that are new every morning. Read Philippians 4:4–8, 11–13, 19 aloud.

Sleep: go to bed by half past ten.

DAY 4

Upon Waking

Prayer: thank God because this is the day the Lord has made. Rejoice and be glad in it. Thank Him for the breath in your lungs and the life in your body. Read Matthew 6:9–13 aloud.

Purpose: ask the Lord to give you an opportunity to add significance to someone's life today. Watch for that opportunity. Ask God to use you this day for His intended purpose.

Advanced hygiene: follow the advanced hygiene recommendations from Day 1.

Reduce toxins: follow the recommendations for reducing toxins from Day 1.

Supplements: take one serving of a fiber/green-superfood powder mixed into, or five caplets of a super-green formula swallowed with, twelve to sixteen ounces of water or raw vegetable juice.

Exercise: perform functional fitness exercises for five to fifteen minutes or spend five to fifteen minutes on a mini-trampoline. Finish with five to ten minutes of deep-breathing exercises. (One to three rounds of the exercises can be found at www.BiblicalHealthInstitute.com.)

Body therapy: take a hot-and-cold shower. After a normal shower, alternate sixty seconds of water as hot as you can stand it, followed by sixty seconds of water as cold as you can stand it. Repeat cycle four times for a total of eight minutes, finishing with cold water.

Emotional health: follow the emotional health recommendations from the morning of Day 1.

Breakfast

Drink one cup of hot or iced green tea with honey.

three soft-boiled or poached eggs

four ounces of sprouted whole grain cereal with two ounces of whole milk yogurt or sheep or goat's milk (for recommended brands, visit www.BiblicalHealthInstitute.com and click on the Resource Guide)

Supplements: take two whole food multivitamin caplets and one capsule of a whole food probiotic formula with soil-based organisms.

Lunch

Before eating, drink eight ounces of water.

During lunch, drink eight ounces of water, or hot tea with honey.

large green salad with mixed greens, avocado, carrots, tomato, red cabbage, red onions, red peppers, and sprouts, adding three ounces of low-mercury, high omega-3 canned tuna

salad dressing: mix extra-virgin olive oil, apple cider vinegar or lemon juice, minced fresh garlic, naturally brewed soy sauce, Celtic sea salt, herbs, and spices together; or, mix one tablespoon of extra-virgin olive oil with one tablespoon of a healthy store-bought dressing

one bunch of grapes with seeds

Supplements: take two whole food multivitamin caplets and one capsule of a whole food probiotic formula with soil-based organisms.

Dinner

Before eating, drink eight ounces of water.

During dinner, drink hot tea with honey.

grilled chicken breast

steamed veggies

small portion of cooked whole grain (quinoa, amaranth, millet, or brown rice) cooked with one tablespoon of extra-virgin coconut oil

large green salad with mixed greens, avocado, carrots, tomato, red cabbage, red onions, red peppers, and sprouts

salad dressing: mix extra-virgin olive oil, apple cider vinegar or lemon juice, minced fresh garlic, naturally brewed soy sauce, Celtic sea salt, herbs, and spices together; or, mix one tablespoon of extra-virgin olive oil with one tablespoon of a healthy store-bought dressing

Supplements: take two whole food multivitamin caplets and two capsules of a whole food probiotic formula with soil-based organisms and one to three teaspoons or three to nine capsules of a high omega-3 cod liver oil complex.

Snacks

Drink eight to twelve ounces of water, or hot or iced green tea with honey.

apple and carrots with raw almond butter

one whole food nutrition bar with beta glucans from soluble oat fiber

Before Bed

Drink eight to twelve ounces of water, or hot or iced green tea with honey.

Exercise: go for a walk outdoors or participate in a favorite sport or recreational activity.

Supplements: take one serving of a fiber/green-superfood powder mixed into, or five caplets of a super-green formula swallowed with, twelve to sixteen ounces of water or raw vegetable juice.

Advanced hygiene: follow the advanced hygiene recommendations from the morning of Day 1.

Emotional health: follow the forgiveness recommendations from the evening of Day 1.

Purpose: ask yourself these questions: "Did I live a life of purpose today?" "What did I do to add value to someone else's life today?" Commit to living a day of purpose tomorrow.

Prayer: thank God for this day, asking Him to give you a restoring night's rest and a fresh start tomorrow. Thank Him for His steadfast love that never ceases and His mercies that are new every morning. Read Romans 8:35, 37–39 aloud.

Body therapy: spend ten minutes listening to soothing music before you retire.

Sleep: go to bed by half past ten.

DAY 5 (PARTIAL FAST DAY)

Upon Waking

Prayer: thank God because this is the day the Lord has made. Rejoice and be glad in it. Thank Him for the breath in your lungs and the life in your body. Read Isaiah 58:6–9 aloud.

Purpose: ask the Lord to give you an opportunity to add significance to someone's life today. Watch for that opportunity. Ask God to use you this day for His intended purpose.

Advanced hygiene: follow the advanced hygiene recommendations from Day 1.

Reduce toxins: follow the recommendations for reducing toxins from Day 1.

Supplements: take one serving of a fiber/green-superfood powder mixed into, or five caplets of a super green formula swallowed with, twelve to sixteen ounces of water or raw vegetable juice.

Exercise: perform functional fitness exercises for five to fifteen minutes or spend five to fifteen minutes on a mini-trampoline. Finish with five to ten minutes of deep-breathing exercises.

Body therapy: get twenty minutes of direct sunlight sometime during the day, but be careful between the hours of ten o'clock in the morning and two o'clock in the afternoon.

Emotional health: follow the emotional health recommendations from the morning of Day 1.

Breakfast

Drink eight to twelve ounces of water.

no food (partial fast day)

Lunch

Drink eight to twelve ounces of water.

no food (partial-fast day)

Dinner

Before eating, drink eight ounces of water.

During dinner, drink hot or iced green tea with honey.

healing Chicken Soup (visit www.GreatPhysiciansRx.com for the recipe)

cultured vegetables (for recommended brands, visit www.Biblical HealthInstitute.com and click on the Resource Guide)

large green salad with mixed greens, avocado, carrots, tomato, red cabbage, red onions, red peppers, and sprouts

salad dressing: mix extra-virgin olive oil, apple cider vinegar or lemon juice, minced fresh garlic, naturally brewed soy sauce, Celtic sea salt, herbs, and spices together; or, mix one tablespoon of extra-virgin olive oil with one tablespoon of a healthy store-bought dressing

Supplements: take two whole food multivitamin caplets and two capsules of a whole food probiotic formula with soil-based organisms and one to three teaspoons or three to nine capsules of a high omega-3 cod liver oil complex.

Snacks

Drink eight to twelve ounces of water.

no food (partial-fast day)

Before Bed

Drink eight to twelve ounces of water, or hot or iced green tea with honey.

Exercise: go for a walk outdoors or participate in a favorite sport or recreational activity.

Supplements: take one serving of a fiber/green-superfood powder mixed into or five caplets of a super-green formula swallowed with twelve to sixteen ounces of water or raw vegetable juice.

Advanced hygiene: follow the advanced hygiene recommendations from the morning of Day 1.

Emotional health: follow the forgiveness recommendations from the evening of Day 1.

Body therapy: take a warm bath for fifteen minutes with eight drops of biblical essential oils added.

Purpose: ask yourself these questions: "Did I live a life of purpose today?" "What did I do to add value to someone else's life today?" Commit to living a day of purpose tomorrow.

Prayer: thank God for this day, asking Him to give you a restoring night's rest and a fresh start tomorrow. Thank Him for His steadfast love that never ceases and His mercies that are new every morning. Read Isaiah 58:6–9 aloud.

Sleep: go to bed by half past ten.

DAY 6 (REST DAY)

Upon Waking

Prayer: thank God because this is the day the Lord has made. Rejoice and be glad in it. Thank Him for the breath in your lungs and the life in your body. Read Psalm 23 aloud.

Purpose: ask the Lord to give you an opportunity to add significance to someone's life today. Watch for that opportunity. Ask God to use you this day for His intended purpose.

Advanced hygiene: follow the advanced hygiene recommendations from Day 1.

Reduce toxins: follow the recommendations for reducing toxins from Day 1.

Supplements: take one serving of a fiber/green-superfood powder mixed into, or five caplets of a super-green formula swallowed with, twelve to sixteen ounces of water or raw vegetable juice.

Exercise: no formal exercise since it's a rest day.

Body therapies: none since it's a rest day.

Emotional health: follow the emotional health recommendations from the morning of Day 1.

Breakfast

Drink one cup of hot or iced green tea with honey.

two or three omega-3 eggs cooked any style in one tablespoon of extra-virgin coconut oil

one grapefruit or orange

handful of almonds

Supplements: take two whole food multivitamin caplets and one capsule of a whole food probiotic formula with soil-based organisms.

Lunch

Before eating, drink eight ounces of water.

During lunch, drink eight ounces of water, or hot or iced green tea with honey.

large green salad with mixed greens, avocado, carrots, tomato, red cabbage, red onions, red peppers, and sprouts, adding two ounces of low mercury, high omega-3 canned tuna

salad dressing: mix extra-virgin olive oil, apple cider vinegar or lemon juice, minced fresh garlic, naturally brewed soy sauce, Celtic sea salt, herbs, and spices together; or, mix one tablespoon of extra-virgin olive oil with one tablespoon of a healthy store-bought dressing

one organic apple with the skin

Supplements: take two whole food multivitamin caplets and one capsule of a whole food probiotic formula with soil-based organisms.

Dinner

Before eating, drink eight ounces of water.

During dinner, drink hot or iced green tea with honey.

roasted organic chicken

cooked vegetables (carrots, onions, peas, etc.)

large green salad with mixed greens, avocado, carrots, tomato, red cabbage, red onions, red peppers, and sprouts

salad dressing: mix extra-virgin olive oil, apple cider vinegar or lemon juice, minced fresh garlic, naturally brewed soy sauce, Celtic sea salt, herbs, and spices together; or, mix one tablespoon of extra-virgin olive oil with one tablespoon of a healthy store-bought dressing

Supplements: take two whole food multivitamin caplets and two capsules of a whole food probiotic formula with soil-based organisms and one to three teaspoons or three to nine capsules of a high omega-3 cod liver oil complex.

Snacks

Drink eight to twelve ounces of water, or hot or iced green tea with honey.

one piece of organic fruit

one whole food nutrition bar with beta-glucans from soluble oat fiber

Before Bed

Drink eight to twelve ounces of water, or hot tea with honey.

Exercise: go for a walk outdoors or participate in a favorite sport or recreational activity.

Supplements: take one serving of a fiber/green-superfood powder mixed into, or five caplets of a super-green formula swallowed with, twelve to sixteen ounces of water or raw vegetable juice.

Advanced hygiene: follow the advanced hygiene recommendations from the morning of Day 1.

Emotional health: follow the forgiveness recommendations from the evening of Day 1.

Purpose: ask yourself these questions: "Did I live a life of purpose today?" "What did I do to add value to someone else's life today?" Commit to living a day of purpose tomorrow.

Prayer: thank God for this day, asking Him to give you a restoring night's rest and a fresh start tomorrow. Thank Him for His steadfast love that never ceases and His mercies that are new every morning. Read Psalm 23 aloud.

Body therapy: spend ten minutes listening to soothing music before you retire.

Sleep: go to bed by half past ten.

DAY 7

Upon Waking

Prayer: thank God because this is the day the Lord has made. Rejoice and be glad in it. Thank Him for the breath in your lungs and the life in your body. Read Psalm 91 aloud.

Purpose: ask the Lord to give you an opportunity to add significance to someone's life today. Watch for that opportunity. Ask God to use you this day for His intended purpose.

Advanced hygiene: follow the advanced hygiene recommendations from Day 1.

Reduce toxins: follow the recommendations for reducing toxins from Day 1.

Supplements: take one serving of a fiber/green-superfood powder mixed into, or five caplets of a super-green formula swallowed with, twelve to sixteen ounces of water or raw vegetable juice.

Exercise: perform functional fitness exercises for five to fifteen minutes or spend five to fifteen minutes on a mini-trampoline. Finish with five to ten minutes of deep-breathing exercises.

Body therapy: get twenty minutes of direct sunlight sometime during the day, but be careful between the hours of ten o'clock in the morning and two o'clock in the afternoon.

Emotional health: follow the emotional health recommendations from the morning of Day 1.

Breakfast

Make a smoothie in a blender with the following ingredients:

1 cup plain yogurt or kefir (sheep's milk is best)

1 tablespoon organic flaxseed oil

1–2 tablespoons raw organic honey

1 cup of organic fruit (berries, banana, peaches, pineapple, etc.)

2 tablespoons goat's milk protein powder

dash of vanilla extract (optional)

Supplements: take two whole food multivitamin caplets and one capsule of a whole food probiotic formula with soil-based organisms.

Lunch

Before eating, drink eight ounces of water.

During lunch, drink eight ounces of water, or hot or iced green tea with honey.

large green salad with mixed greens, avocado, carrots, tomato, red cabbage, red onions, red peppers, and sprouts, adding three ounces of cold, poached, or canned wild-caught salmon

salad dressing: mix extra-virgin olive oil, apple cider vinegar or lemon juice, minced fresh garlic, naturally brewed soy sauce, Celtic sea salt, herbs, and spices together; or, mix one tablespoon of extra-virgin olive oil with one tablespoon of a healthy store-bought dressing

one piece of fruit in season

Supplements: take two whole food multivitamin caplets and one capsule of a whole food probiotic formula with soil-based organisms.

Dinner
Before eating, drink eight ounces of water.

During dinner, drink hot tea with honey.

baked or grilled fish of your choice

steamed broccoli

baked sweet potato with butter

large green salad with mixed greens, avocado, carrots, tomato, red cabbage, red onions, red peppers, and sprouts

salad dressing: mix extra-virgin olive oil, apple cider vinegar or lemon juice, minced fresh garlic, naturally brewed soy sauce, Celtic sea salt, herbs, and spices together; or, mix one tablespoon of extra-virgin olive oil with one tablespoon of a healthy store-bought dressing

Supplements: take two whole food multivitamin caplets and one capsule of a whole food probiotic formula with soil-based organisms and one to three teaspoons or three to nine capsules of a high omega-3 cod liver oil complex.

Snacks
Drink eight to twelve ounces of water, or hot or iced green tea with honey.

apple slices with raw sesame butter (tahini)

one whole food nutrition bar with beta-glucans from soluble oat fiber

Before Bed
Drink eight to twelve ounces of water, or hot or iced green tea with honey.

Exercise: go for a walk outdoors or participate in a favorite sport or recreational activity.

Supplements: take one serving of a fiber/green-superfood powder mixed into or five caplets of a super-green formula swallowed with twelve to sixteen ounces of water or raw vegetable juice.

Advanced hygiene: follow the advanced hygiene recommendations from the morning of Day 1.

Emotional health: follow the forgiveness recommendations from the evening of Day 1.

Body therapy: take a warm bath for fifteen minutes with eight drops of biblical essential oils added.

Purpose: ask yourself these questions: "Did I live a life of purpose today?" "What did I do to add value to someone else's life today?" Commit to living a day of purpose tomorrow.

Prayer: thank God for this day, asking Him to give you a restoring night's rest and a fresh start tomorrow. Thank Him for His steadfast love that never ceases and His mercies that are new every morning. Read 1 Corinthians 13:4–8 aloud.

Sleep: go to bed by half past ten.

DAY 8 AND BEYOND

You can repeat the Great Physician's Rx for High Blood Pressure Battle Plan as many times as you'd like. For detailed step-by-step suggestions and meal and lifestyle plans, visit www.GreatPhysiciansRx.com and join the 40-Day Health Experience for continued good health. Or, you may be interested in the Lifetime of Wellness plan if you want to maintain your newfound level of health. These online programs will provide you with customized daily meal and exercise plans and provide you the tools to track your progress.

If you've experienced positive results from *The Great Physician's Rx for High Blood Pressure* program, I encourage you to reach out to someone you know and recommend this book and Battle Plan to them. You can learn how to lead a small group at your church or home by visiting www.GreatPhysiciansRx.com.

Remember: You don't have to be a doctor or a health expert to help transform the life of someone you care about—you just have to be willing.

Allow me to offer this prayer of blessing from Numbers 6:24–26 NKJV to you:

> The LORD bless you and keep you;
> The LORD make His face shine upon you,
> And be gracious to you;
> The LORD lift up His countenance upon you,
> And give you peace.

Need Recipes?

For a detailed list of over two hundred healthy and delicious recipes contained in the Great Physician's Rx eating plan, please visit www.BiblicalHealthInstitute.com.

NOTES

Introduction

1. Larry Schwartz, "Marino's Golden Arm Changed Game," ESPN, http://espn.go.com/sportscentury/features/00016179.html (accessed March 14, 2007).

2. John Morgan, "Joe Montana Beats High Blood Pressure," *USA Today*, September 30, 2003.

3. Steve Sternberg, "1 in 3 Have High Blood Pressure, Study Finds," *USA Today*, August 24, 2004.

4. Abdou Elhendy, Kerry Prewitt, and Stephen J. Gulotta, eds., "High Blood Pressure," iVillage Total Health, http://heart.healthcentersonline.com/bloodpressure/hypertension.cfm (accessed February 27, 2007).

5. "Am I at Risk?", American Heart Association, http://www.americanheart.org/presenter.jhtml?identifier=2142 (accessed March 28, 2007).

6. Harvey Simon, M.D., ed., "High Blood Pressure," Reuters Health, http://www.reutershealth.com/wellconnected/doc14.html (accessed February 28, 2007).

7. "Medications and Supplements That Can Raise Your Blood Pressure," MayoClinic, http://www.mayoclinic.com/health/blood-pressure/HI00053 (accessed February 28, 2007).

8. "New Hope for Those with High Blood Pressure," Jersey Shore University Medical Center, http://www.meridianhealth.com/jsmc.cfm/MediaRelations/News/HeartCare/sept0105.cfm (accessed February 28, 2007).

9. Harvey Simon, M.D., ed., "High Blood Pressure," Reuters Health, http://www.reutershealth.com/wellconnected/doc14.html (accessed February 28, 2007).

10. William Campbell Douglass, M.D., "Everything You Ever Wanted to Know About Blood Pressure Drugs . . . and How to Avoid Them," Weston A. Price Foundation, http://www.westonaprice.org/moderndiseases/bpdrugs.html (accessed February 28, 2007).

11. "Taking Medication for High Blood Pressure," American Heart Association, http://www.americanheart.org/presenter.jhtml?identifier=2141 (accessed February 28, 2007).

12. Larry Trivieri Jr., ed., *Alternative Medicine: The Definitive Guide*, (Berkeley, CA: Celestial Arts, 2002), 779.

13. Ibid.

14. The Cleveland Clinic Heart Center, "Hypertension: Complementary and Alternative Treatments," WebMD, http://www.webmd.com/content/article/96/103773.htm (accessed March 14, 2007).

Key #1

1. Joe Mercola, M.D., "The Hidden Poison Lurking on Your Kitchen Table," Mercola.com, http://www.mercola.com/forms/salt.htm (accessed March 14, 2007).

2. R. J. Ignelzi, "Pinch the Salt," *San Diego Union Tribune*, September 12, 2006.

3. Rex Russell, M.D., *What the Bible Says About Healthy Living* (Ventura, CA: Regal, 2006).

4. "Food High in Potassium" essortment.com, http://nhnh.essortment.com/potassiumfoodh_rkyn.htm (accessed May 29, 2007)

5. Nichola Groom, "Atkins Files for Bankruptcy as Low-Carb Slumps," Reuters News Service, August 1, 2005.

6. "Omega-3 Fatty Acids," WholeHealthMD.com, http://www.wholehealthmd.com/ME2/dirmod.asp?sid=17E09E7CFFF64044 8FFB0B4FC1B7FEF0&nm=Reference+Library&type=AWHN_Supplement s&mod=Supplements&mid=&id=034025EFA41345DA9594F677FD339F5 5&tier=2 (accessed March 23, 2007).

7. Michael Murray, N.D., Joseph Pizzorno, N.D., and Lara Pizzorno, MA, *The Encyclopedia of Natural Foods* (New York: Atria Books, 2005), 704.

8. "Hypertension," The World's Healthiest Foods, http://www.whfoods.com/genpage.php?tname=disease&dbid=15 (accessed March 14, 2007).

9. Kathleen Fackelmann, "Shake the Salt, Add More Water," *USA Today*, February 12, 2004.

10. Ibid.

11. Jennifer Warner, "FDA OK's Nutty Heart Health Claim," WebMD, http://www.webmd.com/content/article/71/81253.htm (accessed July 17, 2003).

12. Paul Schulick, *Ginger: Common Spice & Wonder Drug*, 3rd ed., (Prescott, AZ: Hohm Press, 1996), 36.

13. F. Batmanghelidj, M.D., *You're Not Sick, You're Thirsty!* (New York: Warner Books, 2003), 95.

14. Jean Carper, "Eat Smart," *USA Today* weekend edition, December 1, 1996.

Key #2

1. Phyllis A. Balch, C.N.C., *Prescription for Nutritional Healing* (Wayne, NJ: Avery Publishing: 2000), 440.

2. Masahiko Hirafuji, Takuji Machida, Naoya Hamaue and Masaru Minami, "Cardiovascular Protective Effects of n-3 Polyunsaturated Fatty Acids with Special Emphasis on Docosahexaenoic Acid," *Journal of Pharmacological Sciences* 92 (2003): 308–316.

3. "High Blood Pressure," Life Extension, http://www.lef.org/protocols/heart_circulatory/high_blood_pressure_02.htm (accessed March 15, 2007).

4. Sharon Linfante, "Reducing Blood Pressure Naturally," Metabolism.com, http://metabolism.com/news/2001-07-04/ (accessed March 15, 2007).

5. Miranda Hitti, "Grape Seed Extract for High Blood Pressure?", WebMD, http://www.webmd.com/hypertension-high-blood-pressure/news/20060327/grape-seed-extract-blood-pressure (accessed March 27, 2006.)

6. C. Kitiyakara and C.S. Wilcox, "Antioxidants for Hypertension," *Current Opinion in Nephrology and Hypertension* 5 (Septermber 7, 1998): 531–38.

7. Heather S. Oliff, Ph.D., "Uncontrolled High Blood Pressure: A Little-Known Failure of Conventional Medicine," *Life Extension* (August 2006), http://www.lef.org/LEFCMS/aspx/PrintVersionMagic.aspx?CmsID=114163 (accessed March 15, 2007).

Key #3

1. Alvin Powell, "C-Reactive Protein, High Blood Pressure Linked," *Harvard University Gazette,* January 8, 2004, http://www.news.harvard.edu/gazette/2004/01.08/11-hyper.html (accessed March 15, 2007).

Key #4

1. Richard H. Grimm Jr., M.D., Ph.D., et al., "Long-term Effects on Plasma Lipids of Diet and Drugs to Treat Hypertension," *Journal of the American Medical Association* 275, no. 20 (May 1996): 1549–56.

2. Associated Press, "Breathing Your Way to Lower Blood Pressure," CNN, August 1, 2006.

Key #5

1. Brunilda Nazario, M.D., ed., "How High Blood Pressure Leads to Erectile Dysfunction," WebMD, http://www.webmd.com/content/Article/116/112107.htm (accessed March 15, 2007).

Key #6

1. Don Colbert, M.D., *Deadly Emotions: Understanding the Mind-Body-Spirit Connection that Can Heal or Destroy You,* (Nashville, TN: Thomas Nelson, 2003), xi–xii.

Key #7

1. Germaine Copeland, *Prayers That Avail Much,* (Tulsa, OK: Harrison House, 1997), 104–5.

About the Authors

Jordan Rubin has dedicated his life to transforming the health of God's people one life at a time. He is the founder and chairman of Garden of Life, Inc., a health and wellness company based in West Palm Beach, Florida, that produces organic functional foods, whole food nutritional supplements, and personal care products and he's a much-in-demand speaker on various health topics.

He and his wife, Nicki, are the parents of a toddler-aged son, Joshua. They make their home in Palm Beach Gardens, Florida.

Joseph D. Brasco, M.D., who has extensive knowledge and experience in gastroenterology and internal medicine, attended medical school at Medical College of Wisconsin in Milwaukee, Wisconsin, and is board certified with the American Board of Internal Medicine. Besides writing for various medical journals, he is also the coauthor of *Restoring Your Digestive Health* with Jordan Rubin. Dr. Brasco is currently in private practice in Huntsville, Alabama.

BHI

BIBLICAL HEALTH
INSTITUTE

The Biblical Health Institute (www.BiblicalHealthInstitute.com) is an online learning community housing educational resources and curricula reinforcing and expanding on Jordan Rubin's Biblical Health message.

Biblical Health Institute provides:

1. "101" level **FREE**, introductory courses corresponding to Jordan's book The Great Physician's Rx for Health and Wellness and its seven keys; Current "101" courses include:

    * "Eating to Live 101"

    * "Whole Food Nutrition Supplements 101"

    * "Advanced Hygiene 101"

    * "Exercise and Body Therapies 101"

    * "Reducing Toxins 101"

    * "Emotional Health 101"

    * "Prayer and Purpose 101"

2. **FREE** resources (healthy recipes, what to E.A.T., resource guide)

3. **FREE** media--videos and video clips of Jordan, music therapy samples, etc.--and much more!

Additionally, Biblical Health Institute also offers in-depth courses for those who want to go deeper.

Course offerings include:

    * 40-hour certificate program to become a Biblical Health Coach

    * A la carte course offerings designed for personal study and growth

    * Home school courses developed by Christian educators, supporting home-schooled students and their parents (designed for middle school and high school ages)

**For more information and updates on these and other resources go to
www.BiblicalHealthInstitute.com**